Adobe® InDesign® CS6: Part 2

Adobe® InDesign® CS6: Part 2

Part Number: 092022
Course Edition: 2.1

Acknowledgements

PROJECT TEAM

Author	Media Designer	Content Editor
John Winter	Alex Tong	Angie French

Notices

DISCLAIMER

While Logical Operations, Inc. takes care to ensure the accuracy and quality of these materials, we cannot guarantee their accuracy, and all materials are provided without any warranty whatsoever, including, but not limited to, the implied warranties of merchantability or fitness for a particular purpose. The name used in the data files for this course is that of a fictitious company. Any resemblance to current or future companies is purely coincidental. We do not believe we have used anyone's name in creating this course, but if we have, please notify us and we will change the name in the next revision of the course. Logical Operations is an independent provider of integrated training solutions for individuals, businesses, educational institutions, and government agencies. Use of screenshots, photographs of another entity's products, or another entity's product name or service in this book is for editorial purposes only. No such use should be construed to imply sponsorship or endorsement of the book by, nor any affiliation of such entity with Logical Operations. This courseware may contain links to sites on the internet that are owned and operated by third parties (the "External Sites"). Logical Operations is not responsible for the availability of, or the content located on or through, any External Site. Please contact Logical Operations if you have any concerns regarding such links or External Sites.

TRADEMARK NOTICES

Adobe® InDesign® CS6: Part 2

About This Course

In *Adobe® InDesign® CS6: Part 1* you were introduced to the many features that help you create professional looking documents. Now you need to create much lengthier interactive documents that need to be accessed across a range of devices. In this course, you will learn advanced InDesign techniques to enhance the look and functionality of your documents.

Using Adobe InDesign, you can create interactive documents and export them for viewing in a web browser with various features such as buttons, page transitions, movies and audio files, hyperlinks and animation. You have the ability to assign color profiles and establish print presets. In creating longer documents, you'll be able to include such features as a table of contents, footnotes, cross-references and an index.

This course is also designed to cover the InDesign CS6 Adobe Certified Expert (ACE) exam objectives.

Course Description

Target Student

This course is intended for students who want to expand their entry-level knowledge of Adobe InDesign by using advanced features and collaboration tools.

Course Prerequisites

To ensure your success, you will need to take the following Logical Operations course:

*   *Adobe® InDesign® CS6: Part 1*

Course Objectives

Upon successful completion of this course, students will be able to use Adobe® InDesign® CS6 to create and deliver professional looking printed and interactive documents.

You will:

*   Create layouts for multiple formats.
*   Manage advanced page elements.
*   Manage styles.
*   Build complex paths.
*   Manage external files.
*   Create dynamic documents.
*   Manage long documents.
*   Publish InDesign files for other formats.
*   Customize print settings.

The LogicalCHOICE Home Screen

http://www.lo-choice.com

The LogicalCHOICE Home screen is your entry point to the LogicalCHOICE learning experience, of which this course manual is only one part. Visit the LogicalCHOICE Course screen both during and after class to make use of the world of support and instructional resources that make up the LogicalCHOICE experience.

Log-on and access information for your LogicalCHOICE environment will be provided with your class experience. On the LogicalCHOICE Home screen, you can access the LogicalCHOICE Course screens for your specific courses.

Each LogicalCHOICE Course screen will give you access to the following resources:

- eBook: an interactive electronic version of the printed book for your course.
- LearnTOs: brief animated components that enhance and extend the classroom learning experience.

Depending on the nature of your course and the choices of your learning provider, the LogicalCHOICE Course screen may also include access to elements such as:

- The interactive eBook.
- Social media resources that enable you to collaborate with others in the learning community using professional communications sites such as LinkedIn or microblogging tools such as Twitter.
- Checklists with useful post-class reference information.
- Any course files you will download.
- The course assessment.
- Notices from the LogicalCHOICE administrator.
- Virtual labs, for remote access to the technical environment for your course.
- Your personal whiteboard for sketches and notes.
- Newsletters and other communications from your learning provider.
- Mentoring services.
- A link to the website of your training provider.
- The LogicalCHOICE store.

Visit your LogicalCHOICE Home screen often to connect, communicate, and extend your learning experience!

How to Use This Book

As You Learn

This book is divided into lessons and topics, covering a subject or a set of related subjects. In most cases, lessons are arranged in order of increasing proficiency.

The results-oriented topics include relevant and supporting information you need to master the content. Each topic has various types of activities designed to enable you to practice the guidelines and procedures as well as to solidify your understanding of the informational material presented in the course. Procedures and guidelines are presented in a concise fashion along with activities and discussions. Information is provided for reference and reflection in such a way as to facilitate understanding and practice.

Data files for various activities as well as other supporting files for the course are available by download from the LogicalCHOICE Course screen. In addition to sample data for the course exercises, the course files may contain media components to enhance your learning and additional reference materials for use both during and after the course.

At the back of the book, you will find a glossary of the definitions of the terms and concepts used throughout the course. You will also find an index to assist in locating information within the instructional components of the book.

As You Review

Any method of instruction is only as effective as the time and effort you, the student, are willing to invest in it. In addition, some of the information that you learn in class may not be important to you immediately, but it may become important later. For this reason, we encourage you to spend some time reviewing the content of the course after your time in the classroom.

As a Reference

The organization and layout of this book make it an easy-to-use resource for future reference. Taking advantage of the glossary, index, and table of contents, you can use this book as a first source of definitions, background information, and summaries.

Course Icons

Watch throughout the material for these visual cues:

Icon	Description
	A **Note** provides additional information, guidance, or hints about a topic or task.
	A **Caution** helps make you aware of places where you need to be particularly careful with your actions, settings, or decisions so that you can be sure to get the desired results of an activity or task.
	LearnTO notes show you where an associated LearnTO is particularly relevant to the content. Access LearnTOs from your LogicalCHOICE Course screen.
	Checklists provide job aids you can use after class as a reference to performing skills back on the job. Access checklists from your LogicalCHOICE Course screen.
	Social notes remind you to check your LogicalCHOICE Course screen for opportunities to interact with the LogicalCHOICE community using social media.
	Notes Pages are intentionally left blank for you to write on.

1 | Creating Documents for Multiple Formats

Lesson Time: 1 hour

Lesson Objectives

In this lesson, you will:

- Build layout variations.
- Link content.

Lesson Introduction

As technology advances, you'll find you have more and more ways in which you can deliver your documents. Gone are the days when print was the only option. Designers must take into account the various formats in which people will access the material. In this lesson you will build layout variations and link content.

TOPIC A

Build Layout Variations

Designers increasingly need to build for multiple device delivery. Adobe® InDesign® has the tools necessary to get this done. There's also some new tools added for CS6 that make the reconfiguring of layouts that much easier. In this topic, you'll build layout variations.

The Page Tool

The **Page** tool can be used to select a master page or layout page that you need to resize, using the **Control** panel to change the settings. Pages inherit their size from the master page they're based on, but you can change the size of the layout page so that it's different from the master.

The Pages Panel

The **Pages** panel displays page thumbnails in various icon sizes for both *document pages* and master pages. It allows you to navigate to pages, and when you move document pages to a new location, the **Pages** panel automatically scrolls to pages that are out of view. The **Pages** panel is used to create, delete, and apply master pages to document pages. You may also insert, move, duplicate, rotate, and delete document pages using the **Pages** panel.

Adding, Deleting, and Moving Pages

To add a document page you can select **Insert Pages** from the **Pages** panel options menu. To create a new page based on a master, click and drag that master page into the document thumbnail area of the **Pages** panel. To delete a page, select it and press the **Delete selected pages** button. To move a page, you need only click and drag that page icon to the new position.

Liquid Layouts

Liquid layouts allow you to design content for multiple page sizes, orientations, or devices. To do this you apply rules to determine how objects on a page are adapted when you change the size, orientation, or aspect ratio. You're able to apply different rules to different pages. Liquid Layout is a general term that covers a set of specific layout rules.

Liquid Page Rules

Liquid page rules are the specific rules you apply to a page to determine how they adapt when resized. You can apply different rules to different pages. Only one liquid page rule can be applied to a page at a time.

There is a set of specific liquid page rules that you can adjust the settings for.

Rule	Description
Scale	All content on the page is treated as a group, and as the page resizes, all elements scale in proportion.
Re-center	All content on the page is automatically re-centered no matter the width. Content doesn't change size.
Guide-based	Guides define a straight line across the page where content can adapt.

Rule	Description
Object-based	You specify liquid behavior for size and location relative to the page edge for each object, either fixed or relative.

Pinning and Locking

When you apply object-based liquid layout rules, you do so by using pins represented by lines that radiate out from all sides of an object and end in a circle. Clicking that circle with the mouse pointer will lock or unlock the size or its position relative to one of the page edges.

Figure 1–1: An example of object–based liquid layout rules applied to size and location using pins.

The Liquid Layout Panel

The **Liquid Layout** panel is another place for you to define the settings for how objects will behave when the page is resized. Each of the four liquid page rules available in the **Liquid Page Rule** drop-down menu offers options specific to that rule.

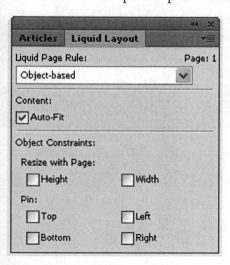

Figure 1–2: The Liquid Layout panel showing the settings for an object–based liquid layout rule.

Alternate Layouts

Alternate Layouts is the feature you'll need if you require different page sizes for print or digital publishing within the same document. For instance, you could build different sizes of the same newspaper advertisement. Another would be to create horizontal and vertical layouts for use with tablets and smartphones.

The Create Alternate Layout Dialog Box

The **Create Alternate Layout** dialog box is available by selecting **Layout→Create Alternate Layout** or from the **Pages** panel options menu. The options it displays are determined by the **Intent** that was selected when you created the document.

Figure 1–3: The Create Alternate Layout dialog box based on a document with print intent selected.

 Access the Checklist tile on your LogicalCHOICE course screen for reference information and job aids on How to Build Alternate Layouts of a Document

ACTIVITY 1-1
Building Alternate Layouts of a Document

Data Files

Flyer.indd

Scenario

You are the graphic designer in the marketing department of the Scrimdown Playhouse. You've already developed a one-page flyer, and now you'd like to adapt it for viewing on devices like the iPad® and iPhone®.

---

1. Open the application Adobe InDesign CS6.

2. Open an InDesign CS6 file.

   a) Choose **File→Open**. Navigate to the folder **C:\092022Data\Creating Documents for Multiple Formats** and open the file **Flyer.indd.**

   b) Make sure rulers are visible by selecting **View→Show Rulers** or typing **Ctrl+R.**

3. Assign Liquid Page rules.

   a) In the **Tool bar**, select the **Page tool** .

   b) In the **Control** panel, in the **Liquid Page Rule** drop-down list, select **Object-based**.

   c) Select the top black rectangle and pin its position relative to the top page edge by clicking the open circle.

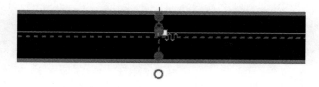

 Note: Use the mouse to view tooltips that define each circle's purpose. Tooltips will also tell you whether the object is pinned/moveable or whether the dimensions are locked/flexible.

   d) Unlock the width of the top black rectangle by clicking the brown circle at far left so that it now appears open.

   e) Select the bottom black rectangle and pin it relative to the bottom page edge, as well as making its width flexible.

   f) Select the image of Shakespeare. Unlock the height and width dimensions so they will resize.

   g) Select the logo image. Pin the right edge relative to the right page edge.

4. Add an alternate layout to the document.

    a) In the **Pages Panel Options** menu, select **Create Alternate Layout**.

    b) In the **Create Alternate Layout** dialog box, verify that the orientation is set to **Landscape** and that in the **Liquid Page Rule** drop-down box, **Preserve Existing** is selected. Select **OK.**

5. Manually adjust the alternate layout.

    a) Reposition or re-size the image of Shakespeare so that it still bleeds off the left edge of the page and it's not underneath the text banner at the top.

    b) Select the text box containing the performance information. In the **Control** panel, in the **Number of Columns** field, type *2*. Reposition the text box as needed.

6. Save and close the file.

 Note: To learn more about digital publishing with InDesign, you can access the LearnTO **Optimize for Digital Publishing** presentation from the **LearnTO** tile on the LogicalCHOICE Course screen.

TOPIC B

Link Content

A key to maintaining consistency and working efficiently is to reuse content where possible. InDesign allows you to re-purpose text and graphics and link them to the original so that you can be alerted of updates. In this topic you will link content.

The Content Collector and Content Placer Tools

The **Content Collector** and **Content Placer** tools allow you to duplicate objects and place them in open InDesign documents. As the objects are collected, they are displayed in the **Content Conveyor** where they can be easily identified and placed as needed.

Place and Link

There is also an option to **Link** these objects within a document or even across any open documents. To do this you may either choose **Edit→Place and Link** or in the **Tools** panel, select the **Content Collector** or **Content Placer** tools.

The Content Conveyor

The Content Conveyor appears when you choose **Edit→Place and Link** or use the **Content Collector** or **Content Placer** tools. The conveyor displays thumbnails of the available objects. Buttons along the bottom provide options to link the content and map styles. There are also settings to have the content disappear after being placed or remain to be placed repeatedly.

Figure 1–4: The Content Conveyor with three objects displayed.

Link Options

Link Options are enabled when an object has been placed and linked. In the **Links** panel options menu, select **Link Options**. There you'll find settings for updates and warning messages. You can also select settings to preserve local edits.

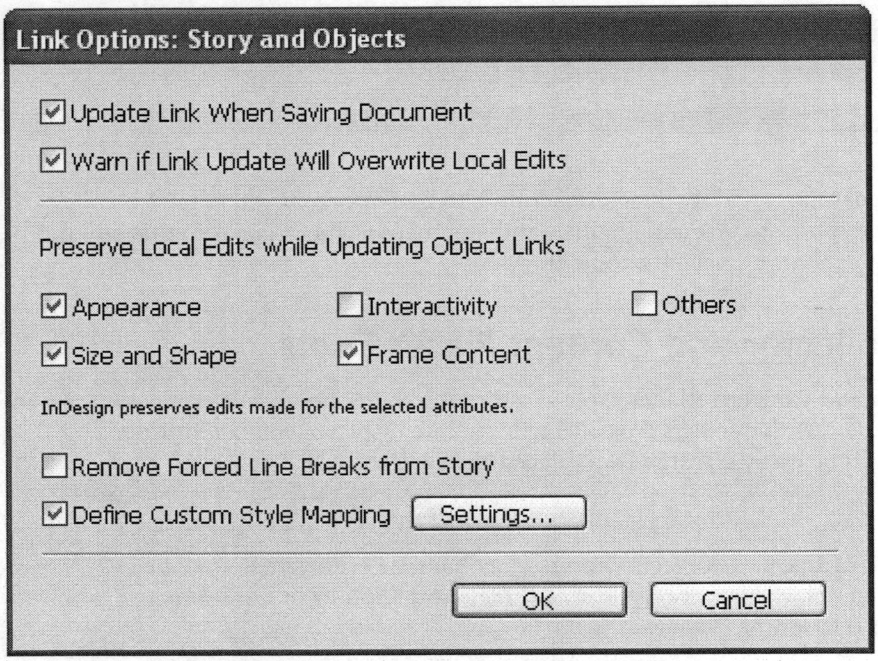

Figure 1-5: The Link Options: Story and Objects dialog box.

Link to Spreadsheet Files

When importing tables from another file, you can maintain a link to the original spreadsheet. When the original file has been edited, a warning in the **Links** panel will notify you that the imported spreadsheet needs to be updated. To do this, select the **Create Links When Placing Text And Spreadsheet Files** option in the **File Handling** preference settings.

Update Links

InDesign notifies you in the **Links** panel when the link to an object is missing or out of date. These links can be identified by the **Modified-link** icon . To update all modified links, you can choose **Update All Links** from the **Links** panel menu. Sometimes a graphic may appear in several places within the graphic. It's possible to just update one instance of the graphic by just selecting the sub link and choosing **Update Link.** Selecting the parent link will update all links to the modified graphic.

Relinking to New Files

You may want to change the source file that the graphic is linked to. To do this, select the **Relink** button or choose **Relink** from the **Links** panel menu. In the dialog box, InDesign lets you browse to the new file to change the link.

Meta Data and File Attributes

In the **Links** panel, at the bottom, you can expand **Link Info** to view a range of file attributes and meta data. This area is not editable but can be useful when you need information about a particular graphic. Some of these attributes are the name, format, page(s) on which it appears, its status, the date it was placed, as well as the date it may have been modified.

 Access the Checklist tile on your LogicalCHOICE course screen for reference information and job aids on How to Link Content

ACTIVITY 1-2
Linking Content

Data Files

Sports Brochure.indd, Business Card.indd

Scenario

You have recently designed a new brochure for a sporting goods store and they're very happy with it. They would like you to redesign their business cards to follow the same style.

1. Navigate to the folder **C:\092022Data\Creating Documents for Multiple Formats** and open the files **Sports Brochure.indd** and **Business Card.indd**.

2. Collect and place content from the brochure into the business card.
   a) With the **Sports Brochure.indd** tab active, in the document window, navigate to page 1.
   b) In the **Tool** bar, select the **Content Collector Tool** ⬚.
   c) With the **Content Collector Tool**, select the text frame containing the text "Getting Where You're Going."
   d) Scroll down and also select the text frame with the logo "my footprint sports."
   e) Verify that these are now in the **Content Conveyor**.

3. Place content in Business card document.
   a) With the **Business Card.indd** tab active, in the document window, navigate to page 2.
   b) In the **Tool** bar, click and hold the **Content Collector** tool to view the tool options fly-out. Select the **Content Placer** tool ⬚.
   c) The **Content Conveyor** window should appear. Click the **Create Link** box to enable it.

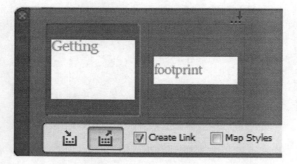

   d) With the mouse pointer loaded with the first conveyor element, click in the pasteboard area to the left or right of the black rectangle. With the **Selection** tool, reposition the text frame "Getting Where You're Going" on top of the black rectangle.

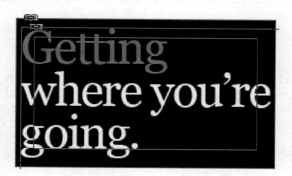

e) In the **Content Conveyor**, verify that the next image is ready for placement.

4. Navigate to page 1. With the mouse pointer loaded with the second gallery element, click in the area above the existing text.

a) Reposition the logo to the top and left margins. Change the text my and sports from white to black.

b) Save the file as *My Business Card.indd*

5. Update linked content.

a) With **Sports Brochure.indd** tab active, in the document window, select the text frame containing the text "Getting Where You're Going." Change the word "Getting" to *Get* and then save the file.

b) With **My Business Card.indd** tab active, in the document window, verify that **Live Preflight** indicates an error at the bottom ● 1 error .

c) Select **Window→Links** to open the **Links** panel. Verify that there are modified links warning icons next to some links. Double-click these icons to update the links in the document.

6. Save and close both files.

Summary

In this lesson, you learned of how InDesign's Liquid Layouts and Alternative layouts can aid in the production of documents that are to be delivered to multiple devices. You also learned that linking content can enable you to repurpose images or text and still link them from the original so that you are alerted of updates to the content.

How can you best take advantage of Alternate Layouts?

When would having linked content be advantageous?

 Note: Check your LogicalCHOICE Course screen for opportunities to interact with your classmates, peers, and the larger LogicalCHOICE online community about the topics covered in this course or other topics you are interested in. From the Course screen you can also access available resources for a more continuous learning experience.

2 | Managing Advanced Page Elements

Lesson Time: 1 hour

Lesson Objectives

In this lesson, you will:

- Create repeating content.
- Work with text layouts.
- Create transparency.
- Use anchored objects.
- Manage a library.

Lesson Introduction

Adobe® InDesign® CS6: Part 1 introduced you to the software and got you started creating documents but there's so much more to discover that can bring those documents to the next level. As a designer, you'll want to spend more time enhancing the formatting of the text in your document as well as possibly include graphic motifs that repeat throughout the document. Additionally, the graphics in your documents can be adjusted to include transparency effects such as drop shadows and embossing and be anchored to flow with the text. Once you've created these graphics, you can build a library to use them in future documents. This lesson will discuss repeating elements, typography, building transparency, anchoring objects and using a library.

TOPIC A

Create Repeating Content

There will come a time as you design when you'll need to make a repeating element in your document that will appear on every page or just certain pages. In this topic, you will step through creating a repeating element in your document.

Master Pages

A *master page* is a page that allows users to define the layout of document pages. It consists of text and images which will appear on multiple pages of a document. All new documents initially contain only one master page, labeled A-Master. Master pages can be edited like any document page. Any change made to a master page will reflect on every document page that is based on that master. Additional master pages can be added and applied to document pages.

Override Master Page

Overriding a master item puts a copy of it on the document page without breaking its association with the master page. Once the item itself is overridden, you can selectively override one or more attributes of the item to customize it. For example, you can change the fill color of the local copy but when changes are made to the copy on the master page, the fill color attribute will no longer update while other attributes like size or stroke will update. Overrides can be removed later to make the object match the master.

 Access the Checklist tile on your LogicalCHOICE course screen for reference information and job aids on How to Repeat Content

ACTIVITY 2-1
Creating Repeating Content

Data Files

Nursery Newsletter.indd

Scenario

You've been asked to develop a monthly newsletter for your daughter's nursery school. Since this will be a regularly updated document, you'd like to take advantage of features in InDesign that allow you to create repeating elements on multiple pages.

---

1. Navigate to the folder **C:\092022Data\Managing Advanced Page Elements** and open the file **Nursery Newsletter.indd**.

2. Create a new master page.
    a) Open the **Pages** panel.
    b) In the **Pages** panel options menu, select **New Master**.
    c) In the **New Master** dialog box, in the **Name** field, double-click and type *Left*
    d) In the **Based on Master** field, select **A-Master**. Click **OK**.

3. Add repeating element to new master page.
    a) In the **Pages** panel, in the master pages area, double-click the master **B-Left** to display it.
    b) In the **Tool** bar, select the **Rectangle Frame** tool and drag a vertical rectangle on the left side of the master. In the **Control** panel, make the **X, Y, W,** and **H** the following: *0, 0, 2.5, 11*. Press **Enter**.
    c) With the rectangle still selected, in the **Swatches** panel, select the **Fill** icon and select the swatch **Dark Green**, if necessary.

4. Create another master page.
    a) In the **Pages** panel options menu, select **New Master**.
    b) In the **Prefix** field, double-click and type *B*
    c) In the **New Master** dialog box, in the **Name** field, double-click and type *Right*
    d) In the **Based on Master** field, verify that **(None)** is selected. Select **OK**.
    e) On master page **B-Left**, select the green rectangle and type *Ctrl+C* to copy it.
    f) Double-click the master page **B-Right** and type *Ctrl+V* to paste it.
    g) With the rectangle still selected, in the **Control** panel, in the **X** field, type *6*
    h) In the **Control** panel, in the **Fill** drop-down menu, select **Nutmeg**.

5. Apply the new master pages.
    a) Right-click the **master page B-Left** and select **Apply Master to Pages**.
    b) In the **Apply Master** dialog box, in the **To Pages** field, type *2,4* and select **OK**.
    c) Right-click the **master page B-Right** and select **Apply Master to Pages**.
    d) In the **Apply Master** dialog box, in the **To Pages** field, type *3* and click **OK**.
    e) Double-click pages 2 through 4 to verify that the repeating element has been added.
    f) Save the file as *My Nursery Newsletter.indd*

TOPIC B

Work with Text Layouts

Text-heavy documents require special formatting considerations. These typographic elements include justification, hyphenation, tracking, and kerning just to name a few. Paying close attention to these details can make a difference in a document's aesthetic appeal.

Hyphenation

Hyphenation is a format that determines whether or not text needs to be broken with a hyphen. You can set the minimum size of a word to be hyphenated, position the hyphen in a word, and determine whether to hyphenate capitalized words or not. You can also control the number of hyphens to be used in a paragraph. Hyphens can be inserted either manually or automatically.

Justification

Justification is a paragraph format that controls the spacing between words and letters in a document to ensure that text margins are evenly spread or appear evenly on the right, left, or both. It also controls the width of characters and the spacing between lines.

Controls word and letter spacing

For the month of November our activities will revolve around Thanksgiving. We will compare the first Thanksgiving and the Thanksgiving celebration of today. We'll talk about different kinds of food eaten for the feast and even do some baking ourselves. Most importantly, we'll focus on family and friends.

For the month of November our activities will revolve around Thanksgiving. We will compare the first Thanksgiving and the Thanksgiving celebration of today. We'll talk about different kinds of food eaten for the feast and even do some baking ourselves. Most importantly, we'll focus on family and friends.

Before justification

After justification

Figure 2–1: An example of text before justification and after.

Keep Options

Keep Options is a feature that allows you to specify the number of lines that you want to retain in a paragraph or heading. The options in the **Keep Options** dialog box let you link adjacent lines of a paragraph and control paragraph breaks. This will prevent text from moving to another column, text frame, or page of a document.

There are different ways to control paragraph breaks using the options in the **Keep Options** dialog box.

Option	Description
Keep with Previous	A check box that, when checked, keeps the first line of the current paragraph with the last line of the previous paragraph.

Option	Description
Keep with Next	A text box that allows you to keep up to five lines together with the last line of a paragraph.
Keep Lines Together	A check box that, when checked, allows you to keep lines of a paragraph together. The options in this section are enabled only when the check box is checked.
Start Paragraph	A drop-down menu that allows you to decide where the reunited paragraph must appear. The options in the drop-down menu are **Anywhere, In Next Column,** and **In Next Frame.**
Preview	A check box that, when checked, allows you to see how the broken lines, such as orphans or widows, are retained with a paragraph.

Widows and Orphans

Widows and *orphans* are words or phrases that are left hanging, or those that are left behind in the text frame when a page or column break occurs. The first line of a paragraph separated by a column or page break is called the orphan line and the last line of a paragraph that is pushed to a new column or page is called the widow line.

Tracking and Kerning

Tracking is a character format that ensures equal spacing between characters in a selected word or paragraph. The spacing is measured in thousandths of an *em*. A positive tracking value increases the space between characters and a negative value decreases the space.

Kerning is a character format that adjusts space between two characters. It can be set either manually or automatically using metrics or optical kerning. *Metrics kerning* depends on *kern pairs* that contain details about spacing between different pairs of characters. *Optical kerning* spaces two characters based on their shapes, and is useful when you are kerning two characters of different fonts. Kerning cannot be applied to more than one pair of characters at a time.

Negative value decreases space   **Positive value increases space**

Figure 2-2: An example of paragraph text with negative tracking and positive tracking values.

Split and Span Columns

InDesign allows you to make a paragraph span across multiple columns in a text frame. You can choose whether a paragraph spans all columns or a specified number of columns. When paragraph spans across columns in a multicolumn text frame, any text before the spanning paragraph will be balanced between the columns that are spanned. You can also split a paragraph into multiple columns within the same text frame. The settings for spanning and splitting columns are available in the **Control** panel or the **Paragraph** panel.

Document Baseline Grid

A document baseline grid is a non-printing grid for aligning columns of text. It appears on the screen as ruled notebook paper and covers the entire spread. It appears on every spread but can't be assigned to any master. It can be made to appear in front of or behind all guides, layers, and objects, but can't be assigned to any layer. Use **Grid Preferences** to set up a baseline grid for the entire document by selecting **Edit→Preferences→Grids**.

Scaling and Auto-resize

Scaling proportionally resizes text in a text frame. When you scale text, the kerning, tracking, and leading values are automatically adjusted, avoiding distortion. To scale text, select the **Scale** tool in the **Tools** panel.

 Access the Checklist tile on your LogicalCHOICE course screen for reference information and job aids on How to Work with Text Layouts

ACTIVITY 2-2
Working with Text Layouts

Before You Begin
My Nursery Newsletter.indd is open.

Scenario
You've created a layout for the nursery school newsletter. Since it is a fairly text-heavy document, you feel that it would benefit from some typographic enhancements.

1. Navigate to page 1 and adjust the view setting to 100%. In the **Control** panel, in the **Workspace** drop-down menu, select **Typography.**

2. Add Kerning and Tracking.
   a) Locate the newsletter heading "greene city nursery school" and with the **Type** tool, place the insertion point between the "r" and the "e" in "green."
   b) In the **Control** panel, in the **Kerning** field , change the value to *-40*
   c) In the **Dates to remember** section, highlight the text **Nov 1 Last tuition payment due.**
   d) In the **Control** panel, in the **Tracking** field , change the value to *-42.* Verify that the word "due" is no longer an orphan on its own line.

3. Add Justification to the body text.
   a) Navigate to page **2** and adjust the view setting to fit screen by typing *Ctrl+0*
   b) Starting with the word "October," highlight all the body text in the two columns.
   c) In the **Control** panel, select the **Justify with last line aligned left** button .

4. Keep first lines of a paragraph with the rest of the paragraph.
   a) Highlight the text "We wish our GCNS families a very Happy Thanksgiving!" and from the **Paragraph** panel options menu, choose **Keep Options.**
   b) In the **Keep Options** dialog box, check the check box next to **Keep Lines Together**, and select **All Lines in Paragraph.**
   c) In the **Start Paragraph** field, select **On Next Page**. Select **OK.**
   d) Verify that the text has been moved to the top of the next page in the document.

5. Save the file.

TOPIC C

Create Transparency

Transparency is a useful tool in adding depth and visual interest to a layout. Drop shadows on text and graphics and the layering of objects with different opacity are just a few examples of how transparency can add to your document. In this topic, you will create transparency.

Transparency

Transparency is a setting that allows you to adjust the opacity of an object. Transparency can be scaled from 0%, where the object is completely transparent, to 100% opacity, where the object is completely solid. Transparency can be applied to text and graphic objects.

The Effects Panel

The **Effects** panel allows you to determine the degree of opacity for an object, stroke, fill, and text. Using the components in this panel, you can specify how colors in transparent objects interact with objects behind them.

Component	Description
Blending Mode	A drop-down menu that allows you to control the way colors of an object blend with the objects beneath it.
Opacity	A text box that is used to specify the opacity percentage.
Isolate Blending	A check box that, when checked, allows you to restrict blending to specific groups of objects and to prevent other objects from being affected.
Knockout Group	A check box that, when checked, allows you to block opacity and blending attributes of every object in the selected group.
Clears all effects and makes object opaque	A button that allows you to clear the effects of an object and makes the object opaque.
Add an object effect to the selected target	A button that allows you to add an object effect to the selected target.
Removes effects from the selected target	A button that allows you to remove effects from the selected target.

Transparency Effects

InDesign allows you to apply various preset transparency effects to objects.

Effect	Description
Drop Shadow	Adds a shadow behind objects, strokes, fills, or text.
Inner Shadow	Adds a shadow that falls just inside the edges of the object, stroke, fill, or text.

Effect	Description
Outer Glow	Adds a glow that emanates from the outer edges of the object, stroke, fill, or text.
Inner Glow	Adds a glow that emanates from the inner edges of the object, stroke, fill, or text.
Bevel and Emboss	Adds various combinations of highlights and shadows to give text and images a three-dimensional appearance.
Satin	Adds interior shading to the object that resembles a satin finish.
Basic Feather	Softens the edges of an object over a specified distance.
Directional Feather	Softens edges of an object by fading the edges from specified directions.
Gradient Feather	Softens specific areas of an object by fading them so that they become transparent.

The following figure shows an example of two transparency effects applied to a shape.

Figure 2–3: An example of transparency effects applied to a colored shape.

Blending Modes

Blending modes control the way colors blend with overlapping objects. You can group specific objects and check the **Isolate Blending** check box in the **Effects** panel to limit blending to specific objects. The blending modes offered in InDesign are the same ones available in Photoshop® and create the same results.

 Access the Checklist tile on your LogicalCHOICE course screen for reference information and job aids on How to Create Transparency

ACTIVITY 2–3
Creating Transparency

Before You Begin
My Nursery Newsletter.indd is open.

Scenario
The side panels you added to the newsletter master pages look a little flat. You decide they would benefit from a drop shadow and a gradient effect.

---

1. In the **Tools** panel, select the **Selection** tool.

2. Apply a drop shadow to the rectangles on the master pages.
   a) In the **Pages** panel, double-click the master page **B-Left** and select the green rectangle.

   b) In the **Control** panel, press the **Effects** button and select **Drop Shadow**.
   c) In the **Effects** dialog box, in the **Opacity** field, change the value to *50%* and in the **Angle** field, change the value to *180* and select **OK**.
   d) Double-click the master page **B-Right** and select the nutmeg rectangle. Select **Effects** and adjust the **Drop Shadow** settings **Opacity** and **Angle** to *50* and *0* respectively.

3. Apply a satin blending effect to the rectangles on the master pages.
   a) With the nutmeg rectangle still selected, select **Effects** and choose **Satin**. In the dialog box, select **OK**.
   b) Double-click the master page **B-Left** and select the green rectangle. Apply the **Satin** effect with the default settings and select **OK**.
   c) In the **Pages** panel, double-click page 2 to display the page and verify that the effect has been applied.

4. Save the file.

> **Note:** To learn more about using transparency with InDesign, you can access the LearnTO **Make Realistic Drop Shadows** presentation from the **LearnTO** tile on the LogicalCHOICE Course screen.

TOPIC D

Use Anchored Objects

Anchored objects are considered best practice when it comes to including graphics in text. InDesign makes this a simple process that you'll find yourself using quite often. In this topic you will anchor objects.

Anchored Objects

An *anchored object* is an object that is linked to a text frame. When you insert an anchored object, an anchor marker is displayed on that object. The anchored object can be a picture frame or a text frame. The anchored object can be positioned inside or outside a text frame.

Inline Graphics

An *inline graphic* is a graphic that appears along with its associated text. When text is edited or formatted, the inline graphic moves along with the text. You can position the inline graphic object below or above the line of text.

 Access the Checklist tile on your LogicalCHOICE course screen for reference information and job aids on How to Use Anchored Objects

ACTIVITY 2-4
Using Anchored Objects

Data Files

turkey.jpg

Before You Begin

My Nursery Newsletter.indd is open.

Scenario

The text of the newsletter has some children's song lyrics that might benefit from an illustration anchored in the text.

---

1. Insert an anchored graphics frame.
    a) Navigate to page **3** and with the **Type** tool, place the insertion point after the text "The Turkey."
    b) Select **Object→Anchored Object→Insert**.
    c) In the **Insert Anchored Object** dialog box, in the **Object Options** section, in the **Content** field, change the selection to **Graphic**. In the **Height** field, change the value to *0.5 in*
    d) In the **Position** field, change the selection to **Inline or Above Line**. Select **OK**.

2. Place a graphic into the anchored graphic frame.
    a) Select **File→Place** and browse to the file **C:\092022Data\Managing Advanced Page Elements \images\turkey.jpg**. Select the file and then select **Open**.
    b) Right-click the image and select **Fitting→Fit Content Proportionally**.

3. Save the file.

TOPIC E

Manage a Library

The Library is a smart tool to take advantage of when creating documents. It helps you organize the graphics, text, and pages you use most often. In this topic you will manage a library.

Libraries

A *library* is a file that is used to store objects that can be used later, either in the same document or in a different one. It stores objects such as rulers, guides, shapes, images, text, and pages. InDesign tracks the location of these objects on the hard drive. When a library object is deleted from the hard drive, it can't be accessed using the library.

 Note: Library files have the .indl file extension.

The Library Panel

The **Library** panel allows you to manage items in a library. It displays library items and their names as thumbnail images. The **Library Item Information** button is used to display and alter information about the selected object. The **Library** panel contains options to search for, add, and delete library items. The **Library** panel options menu displays various commands that can be used to perform operations such as adding items to the library, placing items on a page, updating and sorting library items.

 Access the Checklist tile on your LogicalCHOICE course screen for reference information and job aids on How to Manage a Library

ACTIVITY 2-5
Managing a Library

Before You Begin

My Nursery Newsletter.indd is open.

Scenario

Now that you've completed the newsletter, you'd like to set up a library file to organize the objects you may need to reuse in other documents for the nursery school.

---

1. Create a library.
    a) Select **File→New→Library**.
    b) Navigate to select the location **C:\092022Data\Managing Advanced Page Elements**.
    c) In the **New Library** dialog box, in the **File name** field, type *Newsletter Library* and select **Save**.

2. Add images to the library.
    a) On page **1,** with the **Selection** tool, select the banner image and drag it into the **Library** panel.
    b) Select all the leaf images on the remaining pages and drag them into the **Library** panel.
    c) Close the **Library** panel.

3. Save and close the file.

Summary

In this lesson, you used master pages to create repeating objects in the document. You also learned how to use the typographic features such as justification, hyphenation, tracking, and kerning. Additionally, you learned about splitting and spanning columns, using baseline grids and scaling.

In your experience, were there times that you could have used master pages when you created a document?

Why would you want to make changes to the tracking or kerning of a paragraph?

 Note: Check your LogicalCHOICE Course screen for opportunities to interact with your classmates, peers, and the larger LogicalCHOICE online community about the topics covered in this course or other topics you are interested in. From the Course screen you can also access available resources for a more continuous learning experience.

3 | Managing Styles

Lesson Time: 45 minutes

Lesson Objectives

In this lesson, you will:

- Import styles from Microsoft Word documents.

- Create nested and GREP styles.

- Apply styles in a sequence and manage overrides.

- Redefine styles and break style links.

Lesson Introduction

In Part 1 of this series, you learned how Adobe® InDesign® gives you the ability to create and save formatting for paragraphs, characters, and objects. It goes beyond these of course. InDesign also lets you import styles from Microsoft® Word documents, build nested styles, apply styles in a sequence, as well as redefine and override styles. In this lesson, you will manage styles.

TOPIC A

Import Styles from Microsoft® Word Documents

There will be times when you will be using content originally developed using Microsoft Word. This feature lets you preserve the formatting styles that were applied in Word and import them to InDesign. In this topic, you will import styles from Microsoft Word documents.

The Microsoft Word Import Options Dialog Box

The **Microsoft Word Import Options** dialog box allows you to import different styles, such as paragraph, character, and table styles, from another document and format them in InDesign.

Category	Description
Preset	A drop-down list that allows you to select a defined preset you want to apply.
Include	A section that contains options for importing the table of contents, indices, footnotes, and endnotes.
Options	A section that allows you to include left and right quotation marks and apostrophes instead of straight quotation marks and apostrophes in imported text.
Formatting	A section that allows you to format a document. Some options include the ability to remove formatting, preserve Word formatting, import styles automatically, resolve style conflicts, and customize the import.
Save Preset	A button that allows you to give a name to the defined preset and save the current settings.

The Load Styles Dialog Box

The **Load Styles** dialog box allows you to import paragraph and character styles from an InDesign document. There are various components that deal with the imported and existing styles of a document.

Component	Description
Incoming Style	The options that display various paragraph and character styles of a document you want to import.
Conflict with Existing Style	The options that allow you to overwrite or rename the imported style if an existing style has the same name. The **Use Incoming Definition** option allows you to overwrite and apply the current style with the loaded style, and the **Auto-Rename** option enables you to rename the loaded style automatically in the current document.
Check All	A button that allows you to check all the styles under the **Incoming Styles** column and to display the corresponding styles under the **Conflict with Existing Style** column.
Uncheck All	A button that allows you to uncheck all the styles under the **Incoming Styles** column.

Component	Description
Incoming Style Definition	A section that allows you to view the attributes of styles.
Existing Style Definition	A section that allows you to view different styles of an existing file. It also enables you to compare the incoming and existing formatting attributes of styles.

Custom Style Mapping

Text styles (paragraph, character, table, and cell) or style groups can be mapped to different styles while linking. In the **Link Options** dialog box, accessed on the **Links** panel, enable **Define Custom Style Mapping** and then select **Settings.** Custom style mapping comes in handy, for example, when you want to use sans serif fonts for digital and serif fonts for print publications. Or, when you want to vary the text style between the horizontal and vertical layouts.

 Access the Checklist tile on your LogicalCHOICE course screen for reference information and job aids on **How to Import Styles from Microsoft Word Documents**

ACTIVITY 3-1
Importing Styles from Microsoft Word Documents

Data Files
Nursery Newsletter Lesson 3.indd, power struggles.doc

Scenario
The latest newsletter for the Nursery School is close to being completed but you've just received some last minute additions. You need to import the content from a Microsoft Word document.

---

1. Navigate to the folder **C:\092022Data\Managing Styles** and open the **Nursery Newsletter Lesson 3.indd** file.

2. Import content from the Word document into the newsletter.
   a) Select the **Type** tool and on page **5**, click in the text frame at top left.
   b) Choose **File→Place** and in the **Place** dialog box, navigate to the **C:\092022Data\Managing Styles**, select **power struggles**, making sure to click the **Show Import Options** check box. Select **Open**.

3. Map the styles in the Word document to the styles in the InDesign document.
   a) In the **Microsoft Word Import Options (power struggles.doc)** dialog box, in the **Formatting** section, verify that the **Preserve Styles and Formatting from Text and Tables** option is selected.
   b) From the **Manual Page Breaks** drop-down list, select **Convert to Column Breaks**.
   c) Select the **Customize Style Import** option to enable the **Style Mapping** button, and select **Style Mapping**.
   d) In the **Style Mapping** dialog box, to the right of **Text body**, in the **InDesign Style** column, select **[New Paragraph Style]**. From the drop-down list, select **Body**.

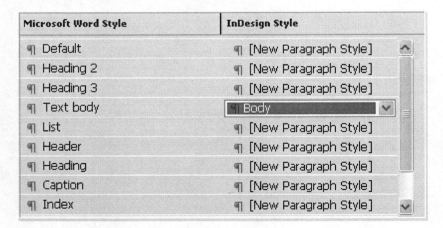

Microsoft Word Style	InDesign Style
¶ Default	¶ [New Paragraph Style]
¶ Heading 2	¶ [New Paragraph Style]
¶ Heading 3	¶ [New Paragraph Style]
¶ Text body	¶ Body
¶ List	¶ [New Paragraph Style]
¶ Header	¶ [New Paragraph Style]
¶ Heading	¶ [New Paragraph Style]
¶ Caption	¶ [New Paragraph Style]
¶ Index	¶ [New Paragraph Style]

   e) To the right of **Heading**, in the **InDesign Style** column, from the drop-down list, select **Subheading**. Select **OK**.
   f) In the **Microsoft Word Import Options (power struggles.doc)** dialog box, select **OK**.

4. Flow imported text into the InDesign text frame.
   a) With the loaded mouse pointer, click in the text frame on page **5**.

b) Verify that the imported text has the **Paragraph Styles** applied to it.

5. Save the file as *My Nursery Newsletter Lesson 3.indd*

TOPIC B

Create Nested and GREP Styles

Nested styles let you apply a sequence of character styles to a paragraph. InDesign also provides a way to format text that conforms to GREP expressions. In this topic, you will create nested and GREP styles.

Nested Styles

A *nested style* is a style that can be applied to specific ranges of text in a paragraph. Nested styles enable you to specify formatting to each character of text separately. They can be applied in different ways to a specified number of lines or sentences. Two or more nested styles can be specified to text. A sequence of nested styles, called nested style looping, can also be applied.

GREP Styles

GREP is an advanced, pattern-based search technique. You can use GREP styles to apply a character style to text that conforms to the GREP expression you specify. For example, suppose you want to apply a character style to all the phone numbers in text. When you create a GREP style, you select the character style and specify the GREP expression. All paragraph text that matches the GREP expression is formatted with the character style.

 Access the Checklist tile on your LogicalCHOICE course screen for reference information and job aids on How to Create Nested Styles and GREP Styles

ACTIVITY 3–2
Creating Nested Styles

Before You Begin
My Nursery Newsletter Lesson 3.indd is open.

Scenario
While working on the formatting of the newsletter you felt that repeatedly bolding the beginning of each calendar entry was tedious. You decide to take advantage of the nested styles feature as a time saver.

---

1. Create a **Character Style** to apply in the calendar section.
   a) Navigate to page **1** and place the insertion point after the colon in the first calendar entry.
   b) In the **Character Styles** panel, select **Create new style** .
   c) Double-click **Character Style 1**. In the **Character Style Options** dialog box, in the **Style Name** field, type *Calendar Bold*
   d) With **Basic Character Formats** selected in the left pane, in the **Font Family** drop-down list, select **Helvetica Neue**. In the **Font Style** drop-down list, select **75 Bold**.
   e) In the **Size** drop-down list, select **11 pt**, and in the **Leading** drop-down list, select **Auto**.
   f) With **Character Color** selected in the left pane, in the swatches list, scroll down and select **Nutmeg** and select **OK**.

2. Create a nested style.
   a) In the **Paragraph Styles** panel, double-click the style **Calendar Item**.
   b) In the left pane, select **Drop Caps and Nested Styles**.
   c) In the **Nested Styles** section, select **New Nested Style**.
   d) In the far left drop-down list, select **[None]** and select **Calendar Bold** (the style you just created).
   e) In the far right drop-down list, select **Words** and type *:* (colon). Click **OK**.

Calendar Bold	through	1	:

   f) Verify that the month in each calendar entry is now bold.

3. Save the file.

TOPIC C

Apply Styles in a Sequence and Manage Overrides

The ability to define styles that are to be assigned in sequential order is a useful feature in InDesign. You can also override a style that's been applied to a paragraph. In this topic you will apply styles in a sequence and manage overrides.

Next Style

Next style is a formatting style that can be applied to text that follows the text to which a style is already applied. This style allows you to organize multiple paragraph styles in a sequence and apply them one after the other to subsequent paragraphs. Next styles are effective when a long document, such as a newspaper or magazine needs to be formatted in a predefined order.

> Access the Checklist tile on your LogicalCHOICE course screen for reference information and job aids on **How to Apply Styles in a Sequence**

Style Overrides

When a style is applied, text is formatted according to the defined style. *Style override* is a feature that is used when the format of a particular portion of text needs to be changed. When this feature is used, the new format applied to the selected portion of text overrides its existing style. The plus sign (+) next to the style name indicates that a style override is applied to the text.

> Access the Checklist tile on your LogicalCHOICE course screen for reference information and job aids on **How to Remove a Paragraph Style Override**

ACTIVITY 3-3
Applying Styles in a Sequence

Before You Begin
My Nursery Newsletter Lesson 3.indd is open.

Scenario
The newsletters will all feature the lyrics to the song that the children will be learning that month. In an effort to streamline the formatting of the song title, artist, and lyrics, you decide to use the Next Style feature within Paragraph Styles.

1. Define the next style sequence for formatting the song on page **3**.
   a) In the **Tools** panel, select the **Type** tool.
   b) In the **Paragraph Styles** panel, double-click **Song Title**.
   c) In the **Paragraph Style Options** dialog box, in the **General** section, from the **Next Style** drop-down list, select **Artist** and select **OK**.
   d) In the **Paragraph Styles** panel, double-click **Artist**.
   e) In the **Paragraph Style Options** dialog box, in the **General** section, from the **Next Style** drop-down list, select **Lyrics** and select **OK**.
   f) In the **Paragraph Styles** panel, double-click **Lyrics**.
   g) In the **Paragraph Style Options** dialog box, in the **General** section, from the **Next Style** drop-down list, verify that **Same style** is selected and select **OK**.

2. Apply the styles in a sequence.
   a) On the nutmeg right panel, place the text insertion point in front of the word "Five." Hold down the **Shift** key and click with the mouse pointer at the end of the last sentence after the text "Day."
   b) In the **Paragraph Styles** panel, right-click **Song Title** and choose **Apply "Song Title" then Next Style**.
   c) Click outside of the text frame to deselect the text. Verify that the styles have been applied in sequence.

3. Save the file.

TOPIC D

Redefine Styles and Break Style Links

Once you have defined the settings of a given style, you are not locked in to those settings. InDesign lets you make adjustments to existing styles as well as break links to styles. In this topic, you will redefine styles and break style links.

Style Redefining

Style redefining is a feature that allows you to redefine character or paragraph style attributes in a document. Styles are a set of style formats that allow you to create and apply text formatting. Using this style, changes to the formatting of the selected text can be applied so that they match the formatting of the text that was already changed.

 Access the Checklist tile on your LogicalCHOICE course screen for reference information and job aids on How to Redefine Paragraph Styles

The Break Link to Style Command

The **Break Link to Style** command allows you to break the link between the paragraph, character, table, and cell styles of the source document and the destination document. When the link of a style is broken, modifying the formatting styles in the source document will not affect the style of the destination document.

 Access the Checklist tile on your LogicalCHOICE course screen for reference information and job aids on How to Break the Link to Text Styles

ACTIVITY 3–4
Redefining Styles

Before You Begin
My Nursery Newsletter Lesson 3.indd is open.

Scenario
The formatting you applied to the song in the newsletter needs some adjustments. The italicized lyrics are hard to read on the dark background and you'd like to change the font style.

---

1. Redefine the paragraph style applied to the song lyrics.
   a) Verify that the **Type** tool is selected.
   b) In the text frame containing the song, highlight the lines of text that contain the lyrics starting with the "Five" and ending with "Day."
   c) In the **Control** panel, from the **Font Family** drop-down list, choose **Helvetica Neue**.
   d) In the **Font Style** drop-down list, choose **55 Roman**.
   e) In the **Font Size** field, type *10* and with the mouse pointer, click in the highlighted text to apply the formatting.
   f) In the **Paragraph Styles** panel, verify that the style **Lyrics** has + (plus sign) next to it.
   g) From the **Paragraph Styles** panel options menu, choose **Redefine Style**.
   h) Verify that the style **Lyrics** no longer has a **+** (plus sign) next to it.

2. Save and close the file.

Summary

In this lesson, you imported styles from Microsoft Word documents, created nested styles, applied styles in a sequence, and redefined a style.

When might you need to create a style based on an existing style?

What are the advantages of creating and then redefining styles?

 Note: Check your LogicalCHOICE Course screen for opportunities to interact with your classmates, peers, and the larger LogicalCHOICE online community about the topics covered in this course or other topics you are interested in. From the Course screen you can also access available resources for a more continuous learning experience.

4 | Building Complex Paths

Lesson Time: 45 minutes

Lesson Objectives

In this lesson, you will:

- Create Bezier paths.
- Create clipping paths.
- Create compound paths.

Lesson Introduction

As part of the Adobe® Creative Suite®, InDesign® offers designers some of the same advanced graphics creation tools that are built into Illustrator® and Photoshop®. The ability to work with paths within InDesign is a convenient, time-saving feature. In this lesson, you will build complex paths.

TOPIC A

Create Bézier Paths

The **Pen** tool in InDesign is based on the industry standard and will seem familiar to Illustrator users. While not a replacement for a full illustration program, it lets you build Bezier paths on the fly and make adjustments to ones imported from other programs such as Illustrator. In this topic, you will create Bezier paths.

Bézier Paths

A *Bézier path* is a path that contains one or more straight or curved line segments. The start and end points of a segment are controlled by anchors. Two other points, called control points, determine the size and shape of the Bézier path. Regular shapes can be modified and converted into Bézier paths.

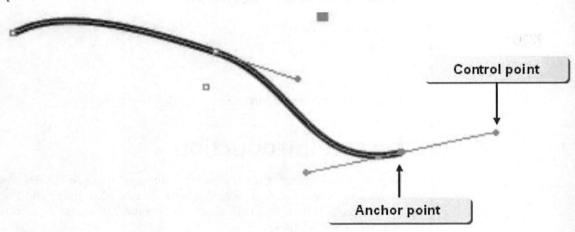

Figure 4–1: An example of a Bézier path showing the anchor points and control points.

Bézier Drawing Tools

Bézier paths are created using the **Pen** or **Pencil** tool. InDesign provides tools that allow you to alter a Bézier path as well.

Tool	Used To
Pen	Draw straight and curved lines.
Add Anchor Point	Add anchor points to a path segment.
Delete Anchor Point	Delete an anchor point.
Convert Direction Point	Convert a corner point to a smooth point and vice versa.
Pencil	Draw a freeform path.
Smooth	Smooth out the surface of a path segment by dragging the tool along the path.
Erase	Delete a path segment.

Text on a Path

Curved text can be created using paths. Text can flow along an open or a closed path. If text exceeds the path, it is hidden from view, which is indicated by a red plus sign (+) at the end of the path. However, you can thread the path to another and display the entire text either above or below the path. When a path's shape is altered, text takes the shape of the altered path. You can apply formatting attributes to the text, alter the stroke value of the path, and hide the path.

Figure 4–2: An example of text on a path.

Type Outlines

A *type outline* is a path constructed by converting the outline of text to a path. The converted text is a set of compound paths that can be edited like a normal path. You can apply color strokes, gradients, or place a picture in the outline that spreads across the compound path. Anchor points can be dragged to modify the shape of the characters. Outlines can also be converted to text frames to hold text.

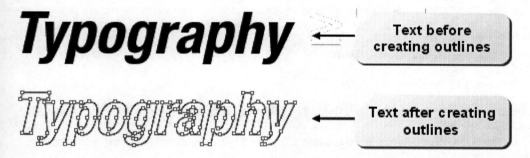

Figure 4–3: An example of type converted to outlines.

 Access the Checklist tile on your **LogicalCHOICE** course screen for reference information and job aids on **How to Create Bézier Paths**

ACTIVITY 4–1
Creating Bézier Paths

Data Files

Nursery Postcard.indd

Scenario

As the publicity chair for Greene City Nursery School, it's your task to publicize the upcoming registration period. GCNS has a large mailing list so you feel a postcard is a good solution. After creating the layout, you decide to add a paint splash graphic behind some of the text.

1. Navigate to the folder **C:\092022Data\Building Complex Paths** and open the file **Nursery Postcard.indd.**

2. Draw a Bezier path.
   a) Navigate to page **1**.
   b) In the **Tools** panel, select the **Pen** tool.
   c) In the **Control** panel, in the **Fill** drop-down list select **Dark Blue**.
   d) In the **Stroke** drop-down list, verify that the selection is **[None].**
   e) Draw a loose shape resembling a puddle of paint that completely covers the text "Open Registration Starts April 24th." Close the shape by clicking on the first anchor point when the mouse pointer turns into a pen with a circle ✎₀.
   f) Choose **Object→Arrange→Send to Back.**

3. Make adjustments to the shape and the text.

   a) Select the shape, if necessary. In the **Control** panel, in the **Effects** drop-down list *fx.*, choose **Bevel and Emboss.**
   b) In the **Effects** dialog box, in the **Structure** section, in the **Style** drop-down menu, verify that **Inner Bevel** is selected. Select **OK.**
   c) In the Tools panel, select the **Selection** tool. Select the text "Open Registration Starts April 24th!" In the **Control** panel, in the **Fill** drop-down list, select **T** so formatting affects the text. And, then choose **[Paper].**
   d) With the mouse pointer, click in the pasteboard area to deselect the text and verify the color.

4. **Save** the file as *My Nursery Postcard.indd* and then close the file.

TOPIC B

Create Clipping Paths

Clipping paths give you the ability to mask off areas of an image and allow other layers below to become visible. InDesign recognizes clipping paths saved in other programs like Photoshop and, on import, lets you preserve these paths. In this topic, you will create clipping paths.

Clipping Paths

A *clipping path* is a path that is used to crop unwanted areas of an image. Though areas of the image outside the path are cropped, areas within the path are visible. The cropped portion is transparent, and other page elements are visible behind that cropped portion. Clipping paths can be created both manually and automatically.

The Clipping Paths Dialog Box

The **Clipping Path** dialog box has options that are used to crop unwanted areas of an image.

Option	Description
Type	A drop-down menu that allows you to choose a path or channel for clipping paths. You can crop images using various clipping path types.
Threshold	A text box that is used to specify the darkest pixel value to define the resulting clipping path and create more transparent pixels. This can be done by increasing the range of lightness values added to the hidden area.
Tolerance	A text box that is used to specify a similar pixel lightness value to the threshold value to avoid unwanted bumps caused by stray pixels.
Inset Frame	A text box that is used to change the size of the resulting clipping path by defining threshold and tolerance values.
Invert	A check box that is used to switch between visible and hidden areas.
Include Inside Edges	A check box that is used to make areas transparent.
Restrict to Frame	A check box that is used to create a clipping path that stops at the visible edges of a graphic.
Use High Resolution Image	A check box that is used to calculate the transparent areas using the actual file for maximum precision.
Preview	A check box that shows a preview of the selected image with its clipping path.

Embedded Clipping Paths

An *embedded clipping path* is a clipping path on an image, which can be imported into InDesign. This path is created using image-editing software other than InDesign. It can be placed and edited in InDesign when it's saved in the TIFF or EPS format. An embedded clipping path can be automatically selected and manually edited; changes can be automatically previewed.

**Before Embedded
Clipping Path**

**After Embedded
Clipping Path**

Figure 4–4: An example of an image with an embedded clipping path.

 Access the Checklist tile on your LogicalCHOICE course screen for reference information and job aids on How to Create Clipping Paths

ACTIVITY 4-2
Creating Clipping Paths

Data Files
Sports Brochure Lesson 4.indd

Scenario
You've added a photograph to the sports brochure but now you feel that it would look better if the background were taken out. You will use the clipping path feature to make this change.

---

1. Navigate to the folder **C:\092022Data\Building Complex Paths** and open the file **Sports Brochure Lesson 4.indd.**

2. Remove the grey background from the running shoe image on page **3** using an embedded clipping path.

    a) Select the running shoe image.
    b) Select **Object→Clipping Path→Options**.
    c) In the **Clipping Path** dialog box, from the **Type** drop-down list, select **Photoshop Path**. Verify that the path selected is **Outline**.
    d) Select **OK** to clip the grey background of the image.
    e) With the **Selection** tool, click somewhere in the pasteboard area to deselect the clipped image. Verify that the background is now invisible.

3. **Save** the file as *My Sports Brochure Lesson 4.indd* and close it.

TOPIC C

Create Compound Paths

InDesign, as in Illustrator, lets you combine multiple paths into compound paths to create unusual shapes with transparent areas. In this topic, you will create compound paths.

Compound Paths

A *compound path* is a path that is obtained by combining two or more simple paths. When several paths are combined, the intersecting area of the paths creates a transparent hole that acts as an object. The fill color of the compound path is the fill color of the backmost object. The fill and stroke of the compound path are common to all the shapes that constitute the compound path. Gradient is applied as a whole to a compound path that is formed by paths that are not overlapping.

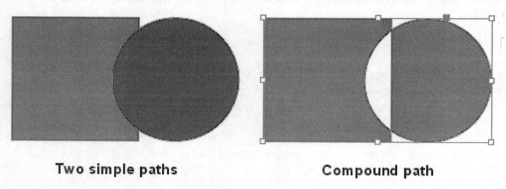

Two simple paths   Compound path

Figure 4–5: An example of how two simple paths can be converted to a compound path.

The Pathfinder Panel

The **Pathfinder** panel is used to combine objects in different ways. It consists of four sections that help you in creating and modifying shapes. They are **Paths, Pathfinder, Convert Shape,** and **Convert Point**.

Paths

The Pathfinder panel contains four buttons pertaining to paths.

Button	Description
Join Path	Used to connect two end points of a path.
Open Path	Used to open a closed path.
Close Path	Used to close an open path.
Reverse Path	Used to change the direction of a path.

Pathfinder

The Pathfinder panel also features five buttons that allow you to work with shapes.

Button	Description
Add	Used to create a compound shape where the intersecting lines are removed.

Button	Description
Subtract	Used to remove the shapes that are displayed in the front from the backmost shape.
Intersect	Used to remove areas that are not intersected by the selected shapes.
Exclude Overlap	Used to exclude the overlapping areas of two shapes.
Minus Back	Used to remove the backmost objects from the areas that intersect with the front-most object.

Convert Shape

The buttons in the **Convert Shape** section are used to convert the existing shape to a different shape. The available shapes include rectangle, rounded rectangle, beveled rectangle, inverse rounded rectangle, ellipse, triangle, polygon, and horizontal or vertical line.

Convert Point

Button	Description
Plain	Used to modify the selected points to have no direction points or lines.
Corner	Used to convert the selected points to have independent directional lines.
Smooth	Used to convert the selected points to form a continuous curve.
Symmetrical	Used to convert the selected points to smooth points that have directional lines of equal length.

 Access the Checklist tile on your LogicalCHOICE course screen for reference information and job aids on **How to Create Compound Paths**

ACTIVITY 4-3
Creating Compound Paths

Data Files
Nursery Newsletter Lesson 4

Scenario
Now that you've added an article about discipline to the latest nursery school newsletter, you'd like to enhance the page with a simple illustration of a sheriff badge. You realize that the simplest and quickest way to create this graphic is by using compound paths.

1. Navigate to the folder **C:\092022Data\Building Complex Paths** and open the file **Nursery Newsletter Lesson 4.indd.**

2. Create a simple path shaped like a star.
   a) Navigate to page **5**.
   b) In the **Tools** panel, click and hold the **Rectangle Frame Tool** , then select the **Polygon Frame Tool** .
   c) With the mouse pointer, click once in the pasteboard area to the left of page **5**.
   d) In the **Polygon** dialog box, in the **Polygon Width** field, type *3*
   e) In the **Polygon Height** field, type *3*
   f) In the **Number of Sides** field, type *5*
   g) In the **Star Inset** field, type *30* and select **OK**.
   h) In the **Control** panel, in the **Fill** drop-down menu, select **Gold**.
   i) In the Tools panel, select the **Selection** tool and then click somewhere in the pasteboard to deselect the star shape.

3. Create a simple circle shape to add to the star.
   a) In the **Tools** panel, click and hold the **Polygon Frame Tool** and select the **Ellipse Frame Tool** .
   b) Click once in the pasteboard area next to the star and in the **Ellipse** dialog box, enter the value *1.5* in the **Width** and **Height** fields, and then select **OK**.
   c) In the **Control** panel, in the **Fill** drop-down menu, select **[Black]**.
   d) Using the **Selection** tool, position the black circle so that it is centered on top of the gold star.

4. Create a compound path from the star and circle shapes.
   a) With the **Selection** tool, click and drag a marque box around the star and circle so that they are both selected.
   b) Choose **Object→Paths→Make Compound Path**.
   c) With the mouse pointer, click the pasteboard area to deselect the compound path in order to verify it.

5. Add text to the sheriff badge graphic.
   a) With the **Type** tool selected, in the **Control** panel, in the **Font Style** drop-down menu, select **85 Heavy**.
   b) In the **Font Size** field, type *24*
   c) With **Type** tool, in the white circle cut-out inside the star, click and drag a text frame and type *Sheriff.* Currently the text is white so it's not visible.

d) With the **Selection** tool, select the text box.

e) In the **Fill** drop-down menu, select **[Black]** and press **Enter**.

f) If necessary, center the word "Sheriff" inside the white cut-out inside the star shape.

g) With the **Selection** tool, drag a marque box around the compound shape and the text frame, and then choose **Object→Group**.

h) In the **Control** panel, change the X and Y values to *3.25* and *.25* respectively.

6. Save the file as *My Nursery Newsletter Lesson 4* and close the file.

 Note: To learn more about complex paths using InDesign, you can access the LearnTO **Use Complex Paths in Custom Graphics** presentation and the LearnTO **Use Type Outlines in a Layout** presentation from the **LearnTO** tile on the LogicalCHOICE Course screen.

Summary

In this lesson, you learned how to create a Bézier path using pen and pencil tools. You also were able to use clipping paths to mask off areas of a graphic. Lastly, you learned how several simple paths can combine to create a compound path.

Describe how you might be able to use compound paths in your layout?

When would a clipping path come in handy?

 Note: Check your LogicalCHOICE Course screen for opportunities to interact with your classmates, peers, and the larger LogicalCHOICE online community about the topics covered in this course or other topics you are interested in. From the Course screen you can also access available resources for a more continuous learning experience.

5 | Managing External Files

Lesson Time: 30 minutes

Lesson Objectives

In this lesson, you will:

- Import layered files.

- Merge data.

Lesson Introduction

As you build a document you'll no doubt have to work with some external files. These may have layers or contain large amounts of data. Adobe® InDesign® allows you to manage the job of including content from these files efficiently. In this lesson, you will manage external files.

TOPIC A

Import Layered Files

When you need to include content from a source file that is built using layers, it's important for you to be able to preserve those layers for use in your InDesign document. In this topic, you will import layered files.

Layer Comps

Layer comps are different versions of an image stored in a file. Layer information of a particular version is stored in a layer comp and minor modifications to multiple layer comps are stored in a single PSD file. While the **Image Import** options dialog box allows you to select a layer comp from a PSD file, the **Show Layers** list box displays a list of layers that belong to the selected layer comp.

Image Import Options

When you import images and check the **Import Options** check box, the **Import Options** dialog box appears with a range of properties.

Section	Description
Image	A tab with a drop-down menu allowing you to select any available clipping path in the target image.
Color	A tab that allows you to define the color profile and rendering intent.
Layers	A tab that displays the layers in the target file and allows you to toggle their visibility when imported into InDesign.

 Access the Checklist tile on your LogicalCHOICE course screen for reference information and job aids on How to Import Layered Files

ACTIVITY 5–1
Importing Layered Files

Data Files
Sports Brochure Lesson 5.indd

Scenario
After looking over the brochure for My Footprint Sports, you realize that you forgot to include the footprint graphic from a Photoshop file. You will import the layered file into the brochure document.

1. Navigate to the folder **C:\092022Data\Managing External Files** and open the file **Sports Brochure Lesson 5.indd.**

2. Create a rectangular frame to place the layered file.
   a) Navigate to page **3.**
   b) In the **Tools** panel, select the **Rectangular Frame** tool and drag to draw a square shape near the bottom of the page underneath the table.
   c) In the **Control** Panel, change the values of **X,Y, W,** and **H** to *9, 8.25, 2.5,* and *2.5,* respectively. Select **Enter**.

3. Import the layered file into the document.
   a) Select **File→Place**.
   b) In the **Place** dialog box, navigate to the **C:\092022Data\Managing External Files\images** folder and select the file **footprints.psd**, verify that the **Show Import Options** box is checked. Select **Open**.
   c) In the **Image Import Options (footprints.psd)** dialog box, verify that the **Show Preview** check box is checked.
   d) On the **Layers** tab, in the **Show Layers** section, select the visibility icon of the **soccer players** layer to turn off its visibility.
   e) Verify that the soccer image is no longer behind the footprints image in the preview. Select **OK**.

4. Save the file as *My Sports Brochure Lesson 5.indd* and close the file.

TOPIC B

Merge Data

When creating such things as form letters, envelopes, or postcards, you'll most likely be merging a data source that contains all this information. You can do this using the data merge feature. In this topic, you will merge data.

Data Merge

Data merge is a feature that is used to merge data from two files—data source and target. Text that is unique to each document is stored in the data source file in the form of a record; text that is the same for all documents is stored in the target file. In addition to this, the target file contains placeholders for the data that will be populated later from the data source file. InDesign places data field values in the placeholders of the target document for each record and stores the record in a new file.

Access the Checklist tile on your LogicalCHOICE course screen for reference information and job aids on How to Merge Data

ACTIVITY 5-2
Merging Data

Data Files

Fundraising Letter.indd, gcns_contacts.csv

Scenario

The chair of the nursery school fund-raising committee has asked you to help out with generating personalized letters to the families. You know that InDesign has a merge feature that will work nicely for this job.

---

1. Navigate to the **C :\092022Data\Managing External Files** folder and open the file **Fundraising Letter.indd.**

2. Specify the data source to merge data in the fund-raising letter.
   a) Select **Window→Utilities→Data Merge.**
   b) From the **Data Merge** panel options menu, select **Select Data Source.**
   c) In the **Select Data Source** dialog box, from the **Files of type** drop-down list, select **All Files.**
   d) Select **gcns_contacts.csv** and select **Open.**

3. Position the data fields to include data in the letter.
   a) In the **Tools** panel, select the **Type** tool and place the insertion point below the text "To:."
   b) In the **Data Merge** panel, select the **Name** field.
   c) Verify that the placeholder appears in the text frame, then press **Enter.**
   d) Similarly, add the **Street, City,** and **State** fields in consecutive lines.

   To:
   <<Name>>
   <<Street>>
   <<City>>
   <<State>>

   e) Place the insertion point after the text "Dear" and press the **Spacebar.**
   f) In the **Data Merge** panel, select the **Title** field and press the **Spacebar.**
   g) In the **Data Merge** panel, select the **Name** field and type **,** (comma) after the insertion.

4. Merge the data to create the letter.

   a) In the **Data Merge** panel, press the **Create Merged Document** button ⬛, to display the **Create Merged Document** dialog box.
   b) On the **Records** tab, in the **Records To Merge** section, verify that the **All Records** option is selected.
   c) Uncheck the **Generate Overset Text Report with Document Creation** check box and select **OK.**
   d) Verify that the placeholders are replaced with data from the source document.
   e) Close the **Data Merge** panel group.
   f) Save the generated letter document as *GCNS Fundraising Letters.indd* and close the file.
   g) Save and close **Fundraising Letter.indd.**

Summary

In this lesson, you learned that InDesign allows you to import a layered external file and turn on and off the visibility of the layers to suit your document. You were also able to see how data from an external file such as a spreadsheet can be merged into a document.

What are the advantages of working with a layered file?

What kind of data would you typically want to merge into your documents?

 Note: Check your LogicalCHOICE Course screen for opportunities to interact with your classmates, peers, and the larger LogicalCHOICE online community about the topics covered in this course or other topics you are interested in. From the Course screen you can also access available resources for a more continuous learning experience.

6 Creating Dynamic Documents

Lesson Time: 30 minutes

Lesson Objectives

In this lesson, you will:

- Create document sections.
- Insert text variables.
- Create interactive documents.

Lesson Introduction

There are features offered in Adobe® InDesign® that allow your documents to become dynamic. These include interactive behaviors, text variables, and automatic numbering to name just a few. In this lesson, you will create dynamic documents.

TOPIC A

Create Document Sections

Assembling a long document may require organizing it into sections. InDesign simplifies this with tools to help with creating sections and automatic numbering. In this topic, you will create document sections.

Automatic Numbering

You can add a current page number marker to your pages to specify where a page number sits on a page and how it will look. Because a page number marker updates automatically, the page number it displays is always correct—even as you add, remove, or rearrange pages in the document. Page number markers can be formatted and styled as text.

Document Sections

A *section* is a portion of a document that holds document items such as index or preface. Different styles of numbering, such as letters of the alphabet or Arabic or Roman numerals, can be used to number the sections. A document can be numbered section-wise, where numbering is restarted at each section. Page numbers can be prefixed to certain characters when numbering a section of a page. You can use either section page numbering or absolute page numbering when printing and navigating to different pages.

Section Page Numbering and Absolute Page Numbering

There are two ways to navigate to different pages: *section page numbering* and *absolute page numbering*. The section page numbering method allows you to access pages by using the page numbers specified for the section. For example, in S1-3, S1 is the section prefix and 3 is the page number. In the absolute page numbering method, the pages are sequentially numbered. If section one has three pages and you want to move to the third page in section two, enter the absolute page number as 6. You can use absolute page numbering even when the section page numbering is used. When both methods are simultaneously used, you have to specify the absolute page number preceded by a plus sign (+).

 Access the Checklist tile on your LogicalCHOICE course screen for reference information and job aids on How to Create Document Sections

ACTIVITY 6–1
Creating Document Sections

Data Files

Sports Brochure Lesson 6.indd

Scenario

The My Footprint Sports Brochure needs to be organized so that the first two pages are considered the introduction to the rest of the document. This will require the use of the sections feature.

1. Navigate to the folder **C:\092022Data\Creating Dynamic Documents** and open the file **Sports Brochure Lesson 6.indd.**

2. Define an introduction section.
   a) In the **Pages** panel, double-click page 2.
   b) In the **Pages** panel options menu, select **Numbering & Section Options.**
   c) In the **Start Section** section, select the **Start Page Numbering at** option and in that field, verify that the value is **1.**
   d) In the **Page Numbering** section, in the **Section Prefix** field, type *B*
   e) In the **Style** drop-down menu, choose **i, ii, iii, iv...** and select **OK.**

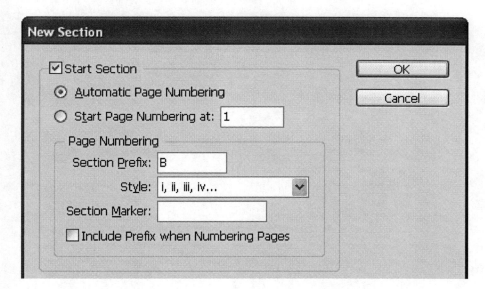

   f) If necessary, select **OK** to close the message about updating chapter numbers.

   Note: In the **Pages** panel, the start of a section is indicated by a black triangle icon above the page thumbnail. Hovering over the triangle icon will give information about that section and double-clicking it will open up the **Numbering & Section Options** dialog box.

3. Define the end of the introduction section.
   a) In the **Pages** panel, double-click page **Biii.**
   b) In the **Pages** panel options menu, select **Numbering & Section Options.**

    c) In the **Start Section** section, select the **Start Page Numbering at** option and in that field, verify that the value is **1**.

    d) In the **Page Numbering** section, in the **Section Prefix** field, type *C* and select **OK**.

    e) Verify in the **Pages** panel that the page thumbnails are reorganized into labeled sections.

4. Save the file as *My Sports Brochure Lesson 6.indd* and close the file.

TOPIC B

Insert Text Variables

Text variables are items that you can place in your document that change based on the context. They're very useful and InDesign has a range for you to take advantage of. In this topic, you will insert text variables.

Text Variables

A text variable is an item that stores text values that can be changed dynamically according to the context in a document. There are different kinds of text variables.

Text Variable	Used To
Chapter Number	Insert chapter numbers.
Creation Date	Insert the date the document was created.
Modification Date	Insert the date the document was last modified.
Output Date	Insert the date on which the document starts as a print job or is exported as a PDF file.
Custom Text	Insert placeholder text.
File Name	Insert the name of the current file.
Last Page Number	Add the total number of pages in a document.
Running Header	Insert the first or last occurrence of the text on the page to which the specified style is applied.

The Text Variables Dialog Box

The **Text Variables** dialog box has options that allow you to perform various functions with variables.

Component	Description
Text Variables	A list box that allows you to select the default or custom variable in order to edit it.
Insert	A button that enables you to insert the default or custom variable.
New	A button that helps you create a text variable.
Edit	A button that allows you to edit the default or custom variable.
Delete	A button that allows you to delete the default variable or custom variable.
Convert To Text	A button that allows you to convert a text variable to text.
Load	A button that enables you to overwrite an existing variable with the loaded variable and to apply its new attributes to the text in the current document.

Component	Description
Preview	A section that allows you to preview a text variable in a document when you select, create, or edit variables.

 Access the Checklist tile on your LogicalCHOICE course screen for reference information and job aids on How to Insert Text Variables

ACTIVITY 6-2
Inserting Text Variables

Datafile
Nursery Newsletter Lesson 6.indd

Scenario
At a recent Greene City Nursery School board meeting, it was suggested that page numbering for the newsletter should also include the total number of pages. You're pretty sure that this will be easy to accomplish using text variables.

1. Navigate to the folder **C:\092022Data\Creating Dynamic Documents** and open the file **Nursery Newsletter Lesson 6.indd**.

2. Insert page numbering on a master page.
   a) In the **Pages** panel, double-click the page **A-Master** to display it.
   b) With the **Type** tool, drag a text frame in the bottom right corner of the page.
   c) In the **Tools** panel, select the **Selection** tool.
   d) In the **Control** panel, in the **Fill** drop-down menu, select **[Black]**.
   e) In the **Font Size** field, change the value to *9* and press **Enter**.
   f) Type the word *Page* and then press the **Spacebar**.
   g) Select **Type→Insert Special Character→Markers→Current Page Number** and press the **Spacebar**.

3. Define a text variable.
   a) Choose **Type→Text Variables→Define**.
   b) In the **Text Variables** dialog box, in the left pane, select **Last Page Number** and select the **Edit** button.
   c) In the **Edit Text Variable** dialog box, in the **Text Before** field, type *of* and then press the **Spacebar**. Select **OK**.

4. Insert a text variable after the current page.
   a) In the **Text Variables** dialog box, click **Insert**. Verify that the last page number variable of 1 has been inserted into the text frame after the current page number "A." Select **Done**.
   b) In the **Control** panel, click the **Align Right** button ![align right] . Position the text frame so that it aligns with the right and bottom margins.
   c) In the **Pages** panel, double-click page **1** and verify that the current page and last page numbers display.

5. Apply page numbering to the other master page.
   a) Double-click the master page **A-Master**, select the **Selection** tool and then select the text frame containing the text variables *Page A of 1*. Press **Ctrl+C** to copy the text frame.
   b) Double-click the master page **B-Right**. Press **Ctrl+V** to paste the text frame in the page.
   c) Select the **Type** tool.
   d) In the **Control** panel, select the **Align Left** button.
   e) Select the **Selection** tool.
   f) In the **X** and **Y** fields, change the values to **.25** and **10.65** respectively. Press **Enter**.
   g) Double-click pages **3** and **5** to verify that they have page numbering applied to them.

6. Save the file as *My Nursery Newsletter Lesson 6.indd* and close the file.

TOPIC C

Create Interactive Documents

In this day and age of fast-moving technology, you can't always get away with creating static documents to engage a reader. InDesign offers a number of ways to insert interactive features like buttons, animations, sound, and videos as you build a document. In this topic, you will create interactive documents.

Interactive Documents

An *interactive document* is a document that contains various interactive elements. You can create an interactive document using a combination of media such as video, animation, text, still images, and more. InDesign has continued to advance its ability to create documents that go beyond print. The various panels and tools in InDesign CS6 have made it possible for designers to create interactive workflow and digital publishing.

Panels for Creating Interactive Documents

There are a range of panels that provide quick access to commonly used tools and features for creating interactive documents.

Component	Description
Timing	A panel that allows you to determine the order of objects for animation instead of following the default order. Based on the page event that was assigned to each animation in the **Animation** panel, the list of animations on the current spread will be filtered. The **Play Together** button in the panel allows you to play multiple animated objects at one time.
Object States	A panel that allows you to not only support the creation of remote rollovers for interactive documents, but also create multiple versions of an object. Any number of versions or states can be created for an object.
Preview	A panel that allows you to preview interactivity and animation of the current selection in an InDesign document without having to switch to a different application outside InDesign.
Media	A panel that allows you to preview SWF, FLV, and MP3 files directly in InDesign without having to switch to another application.
Motion Path	A tool in InDesign CS6 that can be used to quickly create or modify the motion path of an animated object.
Animation	A panel that lets you assign a motion preset to any page item, allowing you to create animations quickly.

The Presentation Mode

The *Presentation mode* enables you to preview an active document as a presentation. In the Presentation mode, the document window switches to the Full screen mode, hiding the application menu and panels. A document cannot be edited in this mode. You can move forward or backward through the document, one spread at a time, using the arrow keys. In this mode, the spread fits to the window proportionally and the extra space around the spread, if any will be displayed in gray by default.

> **Note:** The background color of the **Presentation** mode screen can be changed to white or black by pressing the **W** or **B** keys. To change it back to default gray, press the **G** key.

The Animation Panel

Motion presets are pre-made animations that you can apply to objects quickly. Use the **Animation** panel to apply motion presets and change animation settings such as duration and speed. The **Animation** panel also lets you specify when an animated object plays. You can import any custom motion preset created in Flash® Professional. You can also save motion presets you create and use them in InDesign or Flash Professional.

The Timing Panel

Use the **Timing** panel to change the order of when animated objects play. The **Timing** panel lists the animations on the current spread based on the page event assigned to each animation. For example, you can change one set of animations that occur when the page is loaded, and then change another set of animations that occur when the page is clicked. Animated objects are listed in the order they were created. Animations listed for the **Page Load** event occur sequentially by default. Animations listed for the **Page Click** event are played in sequence each time the page is clicked.

Page Transitions

Page transitions are used to create a visual decorative effect such as a dissolve or wipe in the interactive document when the file is exported in the PDF or SWF format. In InDesign you can apply page transitions directly to individual pages or to all spreads in a single click. You cannot apply transitions to different pages within the same spread or to master pages.

Object Export Options

Object export options are used to specify export parameters required when you export to different formats such as EPUB, HTML, or accessible PDFs. Object export options are applied to text frames and graphic frames, as well as groups. Object export options are specified to individual objects or groups and can override the global export settings. Select **Object→Object Export Options**.

Style Export Tags

Use **Export Tagging** to define how text with InDesign styles is marked up in HTML, EPUB, or tagged PDF output. You can also specify CSS class names to add to the exported content. In EPUB/HTML export, CSS classes can be used to differentiate between slight variations in styling. Class names are required if you are using the option to **Include Style Definitions** and the tags are mapped to the basic styles such as p, h1, and h2; class names are then used to generate style definitions. You cannot preview **Export Tagging** within the InDesign layout, as it only impacts the exported EPUB, HTML, or PDF file. **Edit All Export Tags** lets you efficiently view and modify the mappings in a single dialog box.

The SWF Preview Panel

The **SWF Preview** panel lets you review the animations in a thumbnail view within the panel so that you don't have to leave the InDesign application. It offers a play button, a clear button, and a page selector. There are three preview modes: **Preview Selection**, **Preview Spread** and **Preview Document**.

The Media Panel

Movies and sound clips you add to a document can be played when the document is exported to Adobe PDF® or SWF. Use the **Media** panel (select **Window→Interactive→Media**) to preview a media file and to change settings such as **Play On Page Load, Loop,** and sound.

The Buttons Panel

The **Buttons** panel offers a range of settings for the creation of buttons.

Component	Used To
Name	Specify a name for a button.
Events	Specify the event that initiates the desired action.
Actions	Identify the action to be taken when the event occurs.
State Appearance	Specify the visual state for the button.

 Note: To learn more about interactivity with InDesign, you can access the LearnTO **Create Buttons** presentation from the **LearnTO** tile on the LogicalCHOICE Course screen.

 Access the Checklist tile on your LogicalCHOICE course screen for reference information and job aids on How to Create Interactive Documents

ACTIVITY 6–3
Creating Interactive Documents

Data Files

My Sports Brochure Lesson 6.indd

Scenario

The owners of My Footprint Sports are attending a trade show and would like to have you add some interactive elements to the brochure. You decide to add some animation to the cover page.

1. Navigate to the folder **C:\092022Data\Creating Dynamic Documents** and open the file **My Sports Brochure Lesson 6.indd.**

2. Animate the photo on the cover page.
   a) Navigate to page **1** of the brochure.
   b) With the **Selection** tool, select the photo of the runners.
   c) Select **Window→Interactive→Animation**.
   d) In the **Animation** panel, from the **Preset** drop-down menu, select **Fly in from Left**.
   e) In the **Event(s)** section, verify that the **On Page Load** trigger event is selected.
   f) In the **Speed** drop-down menu, select **Ease Out**.

3. Animate the headline text on the cover page.
   a) Select the text frame containing the headline text "Get where you're going."
   b) In the **Animation** panel, from the **Preset** drop-down menu, select **Fly in from Right**.
   c) Expand the **Properties** section.
   d) In the **Opacity** drop-down menu, select **Fade In**, if necessary.

4. Animate the logo on the cover page.
   a) Select the logo.
   b) In the **Animation** panel, from the **Preset** drop-down menu, select **Fade In.**
   c) In the **Duration** field, change the value to **0.5**
   d) If necessary, in the **Animate** drop-down menu, select **From Current Appearance**.
   e) If necessary, in the **Opacity** drop-down menu, select **Fade In**.

5. Preview the animation.
   a) Select the **Preview Spread** button at the bottom of the panel.
   b) In the **SWF Preview** panel, select the **Play** button to preview the animation.

6. Close the **SWF Preview** and the **Animation** panels.

7. Save and close the file.

Summary

In this lesson, you learned how to organize your document into sections, as well as to insert text variables on document pages and master pages. You also learned about all the interactivity features that can enhance documents exported as PDF or SWF documents.

Under what circumstance would you use text variables in a document?

How would you use interactivity features to enhance a document?

 Note: Check your LogicalCHOICE Course screen for opportunities to interact with your classmates, peers, and the larger LogicalCHOICE online community about the topics covered in this course or other topics you are interested in. From the Course screen you can also access available resources for a more continuous learning experience.

7 | Managing Long Documents

Lesson Time: 45 minutes

Lesson Objectives

In this lesson, you will:

- Create a book.

- Build a table of contents.

- Create hyperlinks and cross-references.

- Generate an index.

- Insert footnotes.

Lesson Introduction

Creating great looking documents is one thing but building a book requires a whole different set of tools and Adobe® InDesign® has them. There are features for configuring the pagination, assembling the table of contents and the index, as well as footnotes and hyperlinks. In this lesson, you will manage long documents.

TOPIC A

Create a Book

Assembling a book involves putting together the basic structure for the content. You need to build a table of contents, insert hyperlinks or cross-references, add footnotes, generate an index, and pay attention to pagination and synchronization. In this topic, you will create a book.

Books

In InDesign, a *book* is a file that consists of a number of individual documents that are merged together. The pages of the documents are sequentially numbered. The table of contents, list of tables, and indices of individual documents are automatically merged when you create a book. The styles and swatches can be synchronized. By default, the first document in the book acts as the style source of the other documents; the style source can be changed as required. You can print either the whole book or selected documents in a book. A book can have up to 1,000 documents and be exported as a PDF document.

Pagination

Pagination is a method by which content in a document is divided into pages according to a specified page size and margin settings. It defines the appearance of content on a page and the flow of content across pages. Pagination is used to identify the beginning and end of content on pages and for adding page numbers to documents. It is often used to number multi-page documents such as books and web pages.

The Book Panel

The **Book** panel contains a list of options to create and manipulate a book.

Option	Description
Add documents	A button that enables you to add documents to a book.
Remove documents	A button that enables you to remove documents from a book.
Print the book	A button that enables you to print either a whole book or only selected documents in a book.
Save the book	A button that enables you to save a book.
Synchronize styles and swatches with the Style Source	A button that enables you to synchronize the styles and swatches of documents with the document set as the style source.
Book	A panel options menu that has commands for exporting a book as a PDF file.

Book Synchronization

When you synchronize documents in a book, the items you specify—styles, variables, master pages, trap presets, cross-reference formats, conditional text settings, numbered lists and swatches—are copied from the style source to the specified documents in the book, replacing any items that have identical names. If items in the style source are not found in the documents being synchronized, they are added. Items that are not included in the style source are left as is in the documents being synchronized. You can synchronize the book while documents in the book are closed. InDesign opens the closed documents, makes any changes, and then saves and closes the documents. Documents that are open when you synchronize are changed but not saved.

 Access the Checklist tile on your LogicalCHOICE course screen for reference information and job aids on How to Create a Book

ACTIVITY 7-1
Creating a Book

Data Files

Continents_Africa.indd, Continents_Antarctica.indd, Continents_Australia.indd, Continents_Eurasia.indd, Continents_NorthAmerica.indd, Continents_SouthAmerica.indd

Scenario

You have been working on a travel book covering all the continents. Each continent was the subject of a document, and now it's time to combine them into the book.

---

1. Create a book file to add documents.
   a) Select **File→New→Book.**
   b) In the **New Book** dialog box, navigate to the **C:\092022Data\Managing Long Documents** folder.
   c) In the **File name** text box, type *My Continents Book* and select **Save**. If necessary, close the **Welcome Page.**

2. Add documents to the book.

   a) In the **My Continents Book** panel, select the **Add documents** button ⊞, and then in the **Add Documents** dialog box, use **Shift+Click** to select **Continents_Africa.indd, Continents_Antarctica.indd, Continents_Australia.indd, Continents_Eurasia.indd, Continents_NorthAmerica.indd,** and **Continents_SouthAmerica.indd.** And then select **Open.**
   b) In the **My Continents Book** panel, verify that the six files appear with their page numbers in a sequence.
   c) Select the **Save the book** button 💾.

TOPIC B

Build a Table of Contents

Long documents require the inclusion of a table of contents. InDesign aids the designer in this task with this feature. In this topic you will build a table of contents.

The Table of Contents

The *table of contents* is an item in a document that helps end users locate information easily. It consists of a list of topics with their page numbers in the order they occur in the document. To create the table of contents, include the paragraph style sheets that determine the text to be included in the table of contents. Character styles can be specified for page numbers and characters between the entry and the number. Entries in the table of contents can be sorted in alphabetical order or according to page numbers. Any number of tables of contents can be created: one for a list of chapters, one for a list of tables, or one for a list of figures used in the document.

The Table of Contents Dialog Box

The **Table of Contents** dialog box contains various options that enable you to format the table of contents.

Option	Description
TOC Style	A drop-down menu that contains the default and custom styles of the table of contents.
Title	A text box that allows you to specify a name for the TOC style you want to create.
Style	A drop-down menu that enables you to select a style for the heading. You can also create a style by selecting **New Paragraph Style** from the drop-down menu.
Style in Table of Contents	A section that allows you to select a paragraph style from the **New Other Styles** list box and include the style in the **Include Paragraph Styles** list box. The **Add** and **Remove** buttons enable you to add and remove paragraph styles, respectively, in the table of contents.
Style	A section that allows you to specify different formatting options for the currently selected styles in the **Include Paragraph Styles** list box using the **Entry Style** drop-down menu. When the **More Options** button is pressed, additional options that help apply character styles to page numbers and organize the table of contents entries in alphabetical order are displayed.
Options	A section that allows you to create PDF bookmarks, replace existing table of contents, and include a table of contents in the Book document and others when the respective check boxes are checked. You can also specify options using the **Numbered Paragraphs** drop-down menu if the table of contents has paragraph styles with numbers.
More Options	A button that provides additional options in the **Style** section and allows you to apply styles to the table of contents in various ways.

Option	Description
Save Style	A button that allows you to save the customized TOC style.

 Access the Checklist tile on your LogicalCHOICE course screen for reference information and job aids on How to Build a Table of Contents

ACTIVITY 7-2
Building a Table of Contents

Before You Begin
My Continents Book is open.

Scenario
People who are helping you proofread your Continents book have mentioned that it's hard to navigate quickly to the different sections. You realize that the book needs a table of contents.

1. Specify a paragraph style for the table of contents.
   a) In the **My Continents Book** panel, double-click the **Continents_Africa** document to open it and navigate to page **1**.
   b) Select **Layout→Table of Contents**.
   c) In the **Table of Contents** dialog box, from the **Style** drop-down menu, select **TOC Title**.
   d) In the **Styles In Table of Contents** section, in the **Other Styles** list box, double-click **Header**.
   e) In the **Style: Header** section, from the **Entry Style** drop-down menu, select **Header**.
   f) Select the **More Options** button.
   g) In the **Page Number** drop-down menu, verify that **After Entry** is displayed.
   h) In the **Between entry and Number** field, double-click to select the current value, click the right arrow button next to it, and from the drop-down menu, select **Right Indent Tab**.
   i) If necessary, in the **Options** section, check the **Include Book Documents** check box and select **OK**.

2. Insert the table of contents into the first page of the first document.
   a) On page **1**, in the top-left corner of the left column, click with the loaded text icon to insert the table of contents.
   b) On page **1**, verify that the table of contents is displayed.
   c) Click outside the frame margins to deselect the frame.
   d) Save the file.

3. Save the book.

TOPIC C

Create Hyperlinks and Cross-References

Designers are now able to take advantage of technology in their documents by inserting interactive features such as cross-references within the document and hyperlinks to external content. In this topic, you will create hyperlinks and cross-references.

Hyperlinks

A *hyperlink* enables users to navigate to another location. When creating a hyperlink, the source and destination of the hyperlink needs to be specified. The source can be text, text frames, or graphic frames. The destination can be a page or a text anchor in the same document, a different document, or a web page. Hyperlinks can be formatted differently from the rest of the content of a document.

The Hyperlinks Panel

The **Hyperlinks** panel enables you to create and edit hyperlinks. The **Create new hyperlink** button is used to create a hyperlink. While the **Go to hyperlink source** button enables you to move to the hyperlink text, the **Go to hyperlink destination** button enables you to go to the destination to which the text is hyperlinked. These options are also found on the **Hyperlinks** panel options menu, in addition to options for setting a new destination for a hyperlink, sorting the list of hyperlinks, and setting the hyperlink options.

 Access the Checklist tile on your LogicalCHOICE course screen for reference information and job aids on How to Create Hyperlinks

Cross-References

When creating an index, if two or more terms have the same meaning, you can create cross-references for those terms to avoid repetition. There are different types of cross-references.

Type	Used To
See	Cross-reference a topic without page references.
See also	Cross-reference a topic with page numbers or sub-entries.
See [also]	Automatically assign correct prefixes to cross-references each time an index is generated.
See herein	Refer to a different sub-level entry for details about the current entry.
See also herein	Refer to a sub-level entry for additional details about the current entry.

 Access the Checklist tile on your LogicalCHOICE course screen for reference information and job aids on How to Create Cross-References

ACTIVITY 7–3
Creating Hyperlinks and Cross–References

Data Files

Travel Documentation.indd

Before You Begin

My Continents Book is open.

Scenario

The book could benefit from a link to a related document on travel. You also see the need to add cross references to other parts of the book.

---

1. Create a hyperlink to another InDesign document.

   a) In **Continents_Africa.indd**, navigate to page **3**.

   b) In the right column, with **Type** tool, highlight the text "Travel Documentation."

   c) Select **Window→Interactive→Hyperlinks** to display the **Hyperlinks** panel.

   d) In the **Hyperlinks** panel, click the **Create new hyperlink** button .

   e) In the **New Hyperlink** dialog box, from the **Link To** drop-down menu, select **File**.

   f) In the Destination section, in the **Path** field, click the folder icon and browse to the file **C:\092022Data\Managing Long Documents\Travel Documentation.indd.** Select **Open**.

   g) In the **Character Style** section, in the **Style** drop-down menu, select **Link** and then select **OK**.

   h) Verify that **Travel Documentation** is now listed in the **Hyperlinks** panel.

2. Create a cross-reference to another page in the book.

   a) Near the bottom of the right column, with the **Type** tool, place the insertion point after the text "desert" and press **Spacebar**.

   b) In the **Hyperlinks** panel, select the **Create new cross-reference** button .

   c) In the **New Cross-Reference** dialog box, in the **Link To** drop-down menu, verify that **Paragraph** is selected.

   d) In the Destination section, in the **Document** drop-down menu, select **Browse** and select the file **C:\092022Data\Managing Long Documents\Continents_Australia.indd.** Select **Open**.

   e) In the list box, select **Subheader** and verify that **Deserts of Australia** appears in the right pane. Select **OK**.

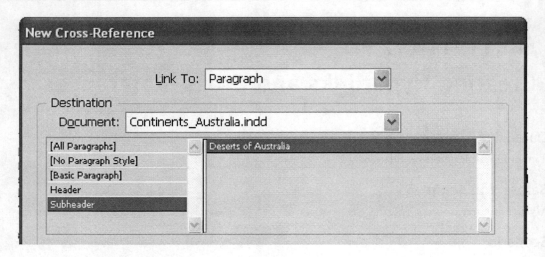

f) Verify that '"Deserts of Australia" on page #' appears in the **Cross-references** section of the **Hyperlinks** panel. Close the **Hyperlinks** panel.

g) Verify that in **Continents_Africa.indd**, page **3**, the text '"Deserts of Australia" on page 25' appears after the text "desert."

3. Save the file.

TOPIC D

Generate an Index

Another feature of long documents and books is an index. The index feature of InDesign offers settings that let you determine how it will be created, what to include, and how it should look. In this topic you will generate an index.

Indexes

An *index* contains a list of words and the page numbers on which these words appear in a document. You can create and organize an index using the Index panel. The words in the index are referred to as topics and the page numbers are referred to as page references. Index entries appear as markers that can be made visible and edited. You can edit an index entry by changing the topic name, creating subtopics, and specifying the range of pages when the topic appears on different pages.

The Generate Index Dialog Box

The *Generate Index* dialog box has various components that allow you to specify a title, as well as paragraph and character styles for the index items. It also allows you to format the created index.

Component	Description
Title	A text field that allows you to enter a heading for the index.
Title Style	A drop-down menu that allows you to select a style for the heading.
Replace Existing Index	A check box that allows you to update an existing index.
Include Book Documents	A check box that allows you to create a single index for all documents in the current book list and renumber the pages of the book.
Include Entries on Hidden Layers	A check box that allows you to include index markers for the entries in a document that appear on hidden layers.
More Options	A button that displays additional index options under sections such as **Level Style**, **Index Style**, and **Entry Separators.**
Index formatting options	A drop-down menu that has options such as **Nested** and **Run-in**. The **Nested** option allows you to format the index in the default style where sub-entries are nested under an entry as separate indented paragraphs. The **Run-in** option lets you format all levels of an entry in a paragraph.
Include Index Section Headings	A check box that allows you to include section headings that have letters of the alphabet.
Include Empty Index Sections	A check box that allows you to include section headings for all letters of the alphabet, even when the index does not have any first level entries.
Level Style	A section that allows you to specify styles for different levels of index entries.

Component	Description
Index Style	A section that allows you to specify a style for the section heading, page number, cross-reference, and cross-referenced topic.
Entry Separators	A section that allows you to specify the separators to be used between entries and between items in each entry.

 Access the Checklist tile on your LogicalCHOICE course screen for reference information and job aids on How to Generate an Index

ACTIVITY 7-4
Generating an Index

Before You Begin
My Continents Book is open.

Scenario
In an effort to make the location of information easy, you decide that you'll also generate an index that will include terms that encompasses the entire book. This will be placed at the end of the last document.

1. Insert index markers into the documents of the book file.
   a) Select **Window→Type & Tables→Index** and in the Index panel, check the **Book** check box.
   b) In the file **Continents_Africa.indd**, on page **4**, select the text "Poisonous Plants" and in the **Index** panel options menu, select **New Page Reference**.
   c) In the **New Page Reference** dialog box, in the **Topic Levels** section, in the first text box, verify that the text **Poisonous Plants** is displayed. Select **Add**.
   d) Select **Done** to close the **New Page Reference** dialog box.
   e) Switch to **Continents_Australia.indd**, page **32** and select the text "Poisonous Plants" and in the **Index** panel options menu, select **New Page Reference**.
   f) In the **New Page Reference** dialog box, in the **Topic Levels** section, in the first text box, verify that the text **Poisonous Plants** is displayed. Select **Add** and then select **Done**.
   g) In the **My Continents Book** panel, double-click **Continents_SouthAmerica.indd** and go to page **62**.
   h) Select the text "Poisonous Plants" and in the **Index** panel, create a new index item as you did for the same text in **Continents_Africa.indd** and **Continents_Australia.indd**.
   i) In the **Index** panel, scroll down and expand the letter **P** and then expand the entry **Poisonous Plants** to display the page numbers that it appears on in the book.

2. Generate an index and place it in a text frame.
   a) In **Continents_SouthAmerica.indd**, add a page to the end of the document.
   b) In the **Index** panel, click the **Generate Index** button ▣ .
   c) In the **Generate Index** dialog box, check the **Include Book Documents** check box, and select **OK**.
   d) Verify that the mouse pointer changes to a loaded text icon.
   e) On the last page of **Continents_SouthAmerica.indd,** click in the left column to load the index.
   f) Verify that the index is placed correctly and that it has one entry under the letter **P** with three page references for that entry.

3. Save the files. Close the **Index** panel.

4. Close the files **Continents_Africa.indd** and **Continents_SouthAmerica.indd**.

5. Save the Book.

TOPIC E

Insert Footnotes

Documenting references in footnotes is essential in composing a long document. The Footnotes feature provides options for collecting and displaying this information in your book. In this topic, you will insert footnotes.

Footnotes

A *footnote* is a note placed at the bottom of a page. It is associated with a specific piece of text on the page. It provides additional information about the text or cites references of the source of the text. The reference mark appears beside the text and the footnote; it indicates the association between them.

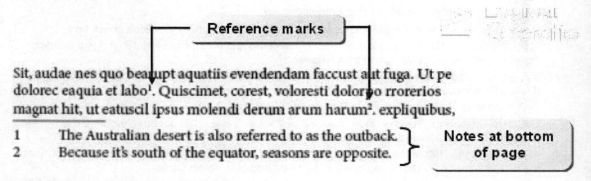

Sit, audae nes quo beaupt aquatiis evendendam faccust aut fuga. Ut pe dolorec eaquia et labo[1]. Quiscimet, corest, voloresti dolorpo rrorerios magnat hit, ut eatuscil ipsus molendi derum arum harum[2]. expliquibus,

Figure 7–1: An example of footnote reference markers with footnotes placed at the bottom of a page.

The Footnotes Options Dialog Box

The **Footnote Options** dialog box allows you to format and modify footnotes. The **Numbering and Formatting** tab in the dialog box contains options that enable you to specify the numbering style of footnotes within a document. This tab enables you to format the footnote reference number using one of the available character styles. You can choose a paragraph style to format the footnote text in the document and specify space between the footnote number and start of the footnote text using separators such as **Em space** and **En space**.

 Access the Checklist tile on your LogicalCHOICE course screen for reference information and job aids on **How to Insert Footnotes into a Document**

ACTIVITY 7-5
Inserting Footnotes

Before You Begin

My Continent Book is open.

Scenario

Because there are so many facts being presented in this book, you decide to add footnotes to each page that requires them. Luckily, InDesign makes this possible with the Insert Footnotes feature.

---

1. Add a footnote to the document.
   a) In the document **Continents_Australia.indd**, navigate to page **25**.
   b) In the left column, in the second paragraph, in the first sentence, place the insertion point after the word "Earth" and before the "." (period).
   c) Select **Type→Insert Footnote.**
   d) Type *Only Antarctica is drier.*

2. Format the footnote.
   a) Select **Type→Document Footnote Options**.
   b) In the **Footnote Options** dialog box, on the **Numbering and Formatting** tab, in the **Numbering** section, check the **Restart Numbering Every** check box. In the drop-down menu, verify that **Page** is selected.

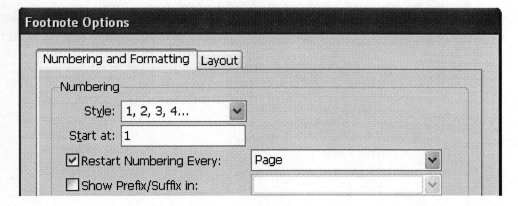

   c) In the Footnote Formatting section, in the **Separator** field, double-click the value to select it. Press the **right arrow button**, choose **Em Space**, and select **OK**.

3. Save and close the document.

4. Save the book and close the **My Continents Book** panel.

Summary

In this lesson, you learned the steps to creating a book. Once the book was developed, you were able to add footnotes, hyperlinks, cross-references, and a table of contents. Finally, you generated an index.

How do you think you'll benefit from the Book feature of InDesign?

Do you know of a way that you will put the hyperlinks feature to use?

 Note: Check your LogicalCHOICE Course screen for opportunities to interact with your classmates, peers, and the larger LogicalCHOICE online community about the topics covered in this course or other topics you are interested in. From the Course screen you can also access available resources for a more continuous learning experience.

8 | Publishing InDesign Files for Other Formats

Lesson Time: 45 minutes

Lesson Objectives

In this lesson, you will:

- Export PDF files for print.
- Export interactive PDF files.
- Export files for animation.
- Export files for web.

Lesson Introduction

As you develop your document you must be cognizant of the various ways in which you many need to deliver it. Printers will require that you export it as a PDF file with printer marks and other necessary settings in place. If your document features interactivity you'll need to know how to export it as an interactive PDF or a SWF file. You should also consider that your document may need to be made available for e-readers in an EPUB format. In this lesson, you will publish Adobe® InDesign® files for other formats.

TOPIC A

Export PDF files for Print

In preparing to export a document for delivery to a commercial printer, there are a number of settings you'll need to consider, such as printer marks, bleed, compatibility, and compression. In this topic, you will export PDF files for print.

Grayscale Output

InDesign CS6 lets you proof and export designs as grayscale PDFs. Use this feature to quickly export your layout for grayscale printing. The digital publication remains full color, and you can avoid maintaining separate layouts for grayscale and color outputs. Use **Proof Setup** (**View→Proof Setup**) to specify grayscale proof options, and choose a **Dot Gain** or **Gamma destination**. After you've setup the proof, select **View→Proof Colors** to toggle between grayscale and color output. You can also export a grayscale PDF from within InDesign. All page items, irrespective of their original color space, are converted to grayscale while exporting to PDF.

Bleed

The **Bleed** area allows you to print objects that are arranged at the outer edge of the defined page size. For a page of the required dimensions, if an object is positioned at its edge, some white may appear at the edge of the printed area due to slight misalignment during printing or trimming. For this reason, you should position an object that is at the edge of the page of the required dimensions a little beyond the edge, and trim after printing. **Bleed** area is shown by a red line on the document. You can set bleed area settings from **Bleed** in the **Print** dialog box.

Printer Marks

Printer marks is the term used to describe all the marks on the document that give information to the printer to ensure proper output.

Printer Mark	Description
Crop marks	Indicate where the page is trimmed. These marks are thin, vertical, or horizontal lines.
Bleed marks	Ensure that colors are printed up to these marks so the color is at the very edge of a page after trimming. These marks look similar to the crop marks, but appear just outside the latter.
Registration marks	Ensure that printing plates align with one another. These marks are not required if the image setter punches holes to align a page.
Color bars	Help the press operator set the density of ink on the press. These appear in gray and colored squares.
Page information	Contains information such as the file name, page number, date, and time.

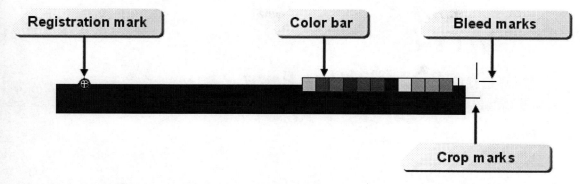

Figure 8-1: An example of a PDF file with printer marks.

Compatibility

In order for users with early versions of Adobe® Acrobat® PDF to access your content, you will need to output to the lowest version of PDF available.

Compression

It is best practice to reduce the file size of documents distributed for viewing purposes only. Text, bitmap images, and line art in a document can be compressed to reduce the size of a file exported to PDF. In the **Export Adobe PDF** dialog box, in the **Compression** area, downsample images to 72 pixels per inch, select automatic compression, and select either low- or medium-image quality for color and grayscale images. When you work with photographic images, use **Automatic (JPEG 2000)** compression; when you work with images that are mostly solid color, such as charts and graphs, use **ZIP** compression.

 Access the Checklist tile on your LogicalCHOICE course screen for reference information and job aids on How to Export PDF Files for Print

ACTIVITY 8-1
Exporting PDF files for Print

Data Files

Flyer.indd

Scenario

The flyer you developed for the Scrimdown Playhouse is ready for the printer. In preparation for that, you want to export a PDF file that includes the necessary printer marks.

1. Create a grayscale output to proof the file before exporting to PDF.
   a) Navigate to the folder **C:\092022Data\Publishing InDesign Files for Other Formats** and open the file **Flyer.indd.**
   b) Select **File→Print**.
   c) In the **Print** dialog box, with **General** selected in the left pane, in the **Printer** drop-down menu, select **Adobe PDF**.
   d) Select **Setup** in the left pane.
   e) In the **Options** section, select **Scale to Fit**.
   f) Select **Output** in the left pane.
   g) In the **Output** section, in the **Color** drop-down menu, select **Composite Gray**. Select the box next to **Text as Black** to enable it.
   h) Select **Print**.
   i) In the **Save PDF File As** dialog box, navigate to the folder **C:\092022Data\Publishing InDesign Files for Other Formats** and **Save** the file as *Flyer_grayscale.pdf*
   j) Open the PDF file and verify that it's a grayscale version of the flyer. **Close** the PDF file.

2. Export the file to PDF with printer marks.
   a) Select **File→Export**.
   b) In the **File name** text box, type **Flyer** and from the **Save as type** drop-down menu, select **Adobe PDF (Print)**, and then select **Save**.
   c) In the **Export Adobe PDF** dialog box, under **General**, in the **Adobe PDF Preset** drop-down menu, select **[Press Quality]**.
   d) In the **Options** section, verify that **View PDF after Exporting** is checked.
   e) Under **Marks and Bleeds,** in the **Marks** section, select the check boxes for **Crop Marks, Registration Marks,** and **Page Information**.
   f) In the **Bleed and Slug** section, if necessary, uncheck the **Use Document Bleed Settings** check box.
   g) In the **Bleed** section, verify that the **Make all settings the same** button ⌷ is enabled. In the **Top** field, change the value to **.25**
   h) Select **Export**. In the **Warning** dialog box, select **OK**.
   i) Verify that the PDF file has crop marks, registration marks, and page information. Close the PDF file.

3. Save and close the file.

TOPIC B

Export Interactive PDF Files

InDesign lets you build PDF files with all the same interactivity that you would if you were using Acrobat. To publish these files you need to export them as interactive PDF files. In this topic, you will export interactive PDF files.

The Export to Interactive PDF Dialog Box

When exporting to an interactive PDF file, you have a range of options to consider.

Component	Description
Pages	A radio button that lets you choose **All**, **Range**, or specific pages.
View	A drop-down menu that offers various view settings.
Layout	A drop-down menu that offers various layout options.
Presentation	A check box that offers the ability to **Open in Full Screen Mode.** With that checked, you are then able to specify the rate at which pages flip.
Page Transitions	A drop-down menu that offers a range of preset page transition animations.
Forms and Media	A radio button that allows you to choose between **Include All** and **Appearance Only**.
Tagged PDF	A check box that gives the option to **Create Tagged PDF**. With that checked, you are then able to check the **Use Structure for Tab Order** check box.
Image Handling	A section containing drop-down menus to specify settings for **Compression**, **JPEG Quality**, and **Resolution**.
Security	A button that displays the Security dialog box with settings for encryption, password, and permissions.

 Access the Checklist tile on your LogicalCHOICE course screen for reference information and job aids on How to Export Interactive PDF Files

ACTIVITY 8-2
Exporting Interactive PDF Files

Data Files
Sports Brochure Lesson 8.indd

Scenario
Since you're already exporting this as an animated PDF, you decide to add some of the other interactive features that Adobe offers such as bookmarks and buttons.

---

1. Create a button to open a coupon.
   a) Navigate to the folder **C:\092022Data\Publishing InDesign Files for Other Formats** and open the file **Sports Brochure Lesson 8.indd**.
   b) On page **3**, select the nutmeg-colored button with the text "Click for Coupon."
   c) Select **Window→Interactive→Buttons and Forms**.
   d) In the **Type** drop-down menu, select **Button**.
   e) In the **Name** field, input the text *Coupon Button*
   f) In the **Actions** section, select the **Add new action for selected event** button ⊕ and select **Open File**. In the **Select File** field, browse to the file **C:\092022Data\Publishing InDesign Files for Other Formats\Sports Coupon.indd** and select **Open**.
   g) In the **Description** field, input the text *Coupon Button*

2. Add bookmarks to the file.
   a) In the **Pages** panel double-click page **1**.
   b) In the **Bookmarks** panel options menu, select **New Bookmark**. In the **Name** field, change the title to *pg1.* Do this for all the pages in the document, naming them appropriately, until there are eight bookmarks.
   c) If necessary, in the **Bookmark** panel options menu, select **Sort Bookmarks** to move them to the same level and in the correct order.

3. Export the file as an interactive PDF file.
   a) Select **File→Export**. Navigate to the folder C:\092022Data\Publishing InDesign Files for Other Formats and in the **File name** field, input the file name *Interactive Sports Brochure*
   b) In the **Save as type** drop-down menu, select **Adobe PDF (Interactive)** and select **Save**.
   c) In the **Export to Interactive PDF** dialog box, select **OK**.
   d) Review the Interactive PDF file and verify that it contains the bookmarks and the coupon button. Close the PDF file. Close the **Bookmark** panel.

4. Save the file.

TOPIC C

Export Files for Animation

InDesign CS6 lets you create animations right in your document and export them to the industry standard SWF file. In this topic, you will export files for animation.

The Export SWF Dialog Box

The Adobe® Flash® Shockwave® (SWF) file format is a vector-based graphic file format for scalable, compact graphics for the web. Vector images are digitally drawn with lines and shapes that allow you to change the image size without distorting the quality. Raster images, also known as bitmap images, are drawn using a grid of small squares or pixels. However, when you drastically change the size of raster images, the edges might appear jagged.

When an InDesign document is exported as a SWF file, the file is ready for playback in Adobe® Flash® Player. The **Export SWF** dialog box has different options that can be used to export an InDesign file as a SWF file.

Tab	Description
General	This tab has a range of sections that can be used to specify certain general settings. These include **Export, Size, Background, Interactivity and Media**, and **Page Transitions**. There is an **Options** check box that displays settings for page curls.
Advanced	This tab has a number of sections that can be used to specify more advanced settings. These include **Frame Rate**, **Text**, and **Image Handling**. There is an **Options** check box that displays settings for interactivity and transparency effects.

The Export Flash CS6 Professional (FLA) Dialog Box

The **Export Flash CS6 Professional (FLA)** dialog box enables you to export an InDesign file as an FLA file. An FLA file is a Flash source file that contains all animations and graphics. An FLA file can be edited using the Adobe Flash Professional application to be viewed in Adobe Flash Player. While an InDesign document is based on pages and spreads, an FLA file is based on video, audio, animation, and complex interactivity. When an InDesign document is exported to the FLA format, each page or spread becomes a separate clip and each will be mapped to a new keyframe. The options in the **Export Flash CS6 Professional (FLA)** dialog box are similar to the options in the **Export SWF** dialog box.

 Access the Checklist tile on your LogicalCHOICE course screen for reference information and job aids on How to Export Files for Animation

ACTIVITY 8-3
Exporting Files for Animation

Before You Begin
Sports Brochure Lesson 8.indd is open.

Scenario
The owners of My Footprint Sports like the opening animation on page one so much that they want to save it as a separate animation for use elsewhere. You know about the InDesign feature that allows you to export pages as SWF files or Flash files so you think you'll look into it.

1. Export the animation on page 1 to a SWF file.
   a) Navigate to page **1**.
   b) Select **File→Export**.
   c) In the **Export** dialog box, navigate to the folder **C:\092022Data\Publishing InDesign Files for Other Formats** and in the **File name** field, type *Cover Animation*
   d) From the **Save as type** drop-down menu, select **Flash Player (SWF)** and select **Save**.
   e) In the **Export SWF** dialog box, in the **General** tab, in the **Export** section, select the **Range** radio button and in the text field, change the value to **1**.
   f) In the **Size (pixels)** section, select **Fit To** and in the drop-down menu, select **800x600** and then select **OK**.
   g) View the SWF playing in the browser window. Click **F5** to replay the animation if necessary, and then close the browser window.

2. Save the file.

TOPIC D

Export Files for the Web

The creation of documents for publishing to the internet or for use on e-readers requires that you export your document with specific settings for use on the web. In this topic, you will export files for the web.

Articles

Articles provide an easy way to create relationships among page items. These relationships are used to define the content to export to EPUB, HTML, or Accessible PDFs; and to define the order of the content. You can create articles from a combination of existing page items within a layout, including images, graphics, or text. Once an article has been created, page items can be added, removed, or reordered. Articles can be created manually by dragging one or more page items to an article in the **Articles** panel.

The Articles Panel

You can manage articles using the **Articles** panel. You can drag page elements into the **Articles** panel to add them to an article. Drag items in the **Articles** panel to change the order, or move them from one article to another. The **Articles** panel options menu provides other options to manage content.

XHTML

*XHTML,*or eXtensible Hypertext Markup Language, is a markup language that is used to display a document in a browser such as Internet Explorer. It is case sensitive and its tags are in lower case. XHTML markup is extensible because it can also be created by the end user.

EPUB

You can export a document or book as a reflowable eBook in EPUB format that is compatible with the Adobe Digital Editions reader software, and other eBook reader software. InDesign creates a single .epub file containing the XHTML-based content. If specified, the exported file may include a cover image. The cover image is created from an image, or created from a JPEG thumbnail image from the first page in the specified document (or the style source document if a book was selected). The thumbnail is used to depict the book in the EPUB readers or the Digital Editions Reader library view. To view the file, you need an EPUB reader.

The EPUB Export Options Dialog Box

The **EPUB Export Options** dialog box contains three tabs offering a range of options.

Tab	Description
General	A tab that offers general EPUB settings. These include **Metadata, Cover, Based On Page Layout, Same as XML Structure, Same as Articles Panel, Book Margin, Bullets, Numbers,** and **View EPUB After Exporting.**

Tab	Description
Images	A tab that offers EPUB image settings. These include **Preserve Appearance from Layout, Resolution, Image Size, Image Alignment and Spacing, Insert Page Break, Settings Apply to Anchored Objects, GIF Options,** and **JPEG Options.**
Contents	A tab that offers EPUB contents options. These include **Format For EPUB Content, Use InDesign TOC Style, Break Document at Paragraph Style, Place Footnote After Paragraph, Remove Forced Line Breaks, Generate CSS, Style Names Only,** and **Use Existing CSS File.**

 Access the Checklist tile on your LogicalCHOICE course screen for reference information and job aids on How to Export Files for the Web

ACTIVITY 8-4
Exporting Files for the Web

Before You Begin
Sports Brochure Lesson 8.indd is open.

Scenario
In order to keep up with the many ways content is being delivered these days, the owners of My Footprint Sports want you to investigate how easy it would be to convert some of the brochure for tablets and eReaders.

---

1. Create an article from the items on page 4.
   a) Navigate to page **4** and select all the text and images on the page.
   b) Select **Window→Articles**.
   c) Drag the selected items from page 4 into the **Articles** panel.
   d) In the **New Article** dialog box, in the **Name** field, type *pg4* and verify that the **Include When Exporting** check box is checked. Select **OK**.
   e) In the **Articles** panel, select **<rectangle>** and click the **Remove** button 🗑.
   f) Reorder the items by dragging them so they are in the following order from top to bottom:

      <Styles that are outside the box...

      <Natetur alibusa...

      <tennis.jpg>

      <Eserum dolupta et,...

2. Export page 4 of the brochure for web.
   a) Select **File→Export**.
   b) In the **Export** dialog box, in the **File name** field, type *pg4* and in the **Save as type** drop-down menu, select **HTML**. Select **Save**.
   c) In the **HTML Options** dialog box, in the **Content Order** section, select **Same as Articles Panel.**
   d) Verify that the **View HTML after Exporting** check box is checked.
   e) Under **Image**, in the **Image Alignment and Spacing** section, verify that the **Align Left** is selected. Select **OK**.
   f) View page **4** of the brochure in the browser window. Close the browser window.

3. Export page **4** of the brochure for EPUB.
   a) Select **File→Export.**
   b) In the **Export** dialog box, in the **File name** field, type *pg4* and in the **Save as type** drop-down menu, select **EPUB**. Select **Save**.
   c) In the **EPUB Export Options** dialog box, under **General**, in the **Content Order** drop-down menu, select **Same as Articles Panel**.
   d) Verify that the **View EPUB After Exporting** check box is checked.
   e) Under **Image**, in the **Image Alignment and Spacing** section, select the **Left Align** button. Select **OK**.
   f) Review the EPUB page in Adobe Digital Editions. Close **pg4.epub**.

4. Save and close **Sports Brochure Lesson 8**.

5. Close the **Articles** panel.

Summary

In this lesson, you learned how the Articles panel can help in organizing page items before exporting documents to HTML or for eReaders.

How does the Articles panel assist in the task of exporting your document for other formats?

What are some of the things you need to consider when you are exporting documents to other formats?

 Note: Check your LogicalCHOICE Course screen for opportunities to interact with your classmates, peers, and the larger LogicalCHOICE online community about the topics covered in this course or other topics you are interested in. From the Course screen you can also access available resources for a more continuous learning experience.

9 | Customizing Print Settings

Lesson Time: 30 minutes

Lesson Objectives

In this lesson, you will:

- Manage colors.

- Preview the print output.

- Create print presets.

Lesson Introduction

As you make final preparations for printing your document, you have a wide range of print settings that you can choose from to customize the printing process to your specifications. You can manage color settings and profiles, preview the print output, and create print presets. In this lesson, you will customize print settings.

TOPIC A

Manage Colors

It's important to review your color settings before handing off the document. Considerations such as color profiles, transparency blend space, and other settings must be reconciled in order to avoid possible delays involving color later on. In this topic you, will manage colors.

Color Management

Color management is the process of matching colors between devices such as a computer monitor and a printer. Color management typically consists of software to profile or characterize each device, and transform the colors in images based on the intended output. Color management may also use hardware to calibrate devices.

Color Profiles

When you enable color management in the Assign Profiles dialog box, you can designate color profiles for RGB and CMYK colors that are applicable to the document. InDesign accepts color management profiles embedded in images and graphics, so the profiles can adjust the color of Adobe® Photoshop® and Adobe® Illustrator® images that were prepared in different color spaces.

ICC Color Profiles

Adobe color management uses ICC profiles, a format defined by the International color Consortium (ICC) as a cross-platform standard. The **Color Management Policies** section of the **Color Settings** dialog box enables you to control profile mismatches.

Spot Colors and Process Colors

A *spot color* is a color that is printed with only one ink. Spot colors are used to replicate colors accurately and consistently. The combination of inks mixed according to the manufacturer's formula and the paper on which the color is printed determines the exact appearance of the spot color.

A *process color* is a color that is printed with four standard inks on four separate plates. It is a combination of the four offset inks: Cyan, Magenta, Yellow, and Black. These are collectively referred to as CMYK.

Transparency Blend Space

If you apply transparency to objects on a spread, all colors on that spread convert to the transparency blend space you've chosen (**Edit→Transparency Blend Space**), either **Document RGB** or **Document CMYK**, even if they're not involved with transparency. Converting all the colors results in consistency across any two same-colored objects in a spread, and avoids more dramatic color behavior at the edges of transparency. Colors are converted as you draw objects. Colors in placed graphics that interact with transparency are also converted to the blend space. This affects how the colors appear on-screen and in print, but not how the colors are defined in the document.

Color Settings

You can set up color management using the **Color Settings** dialog box. The **Settings** drop-down menu provides various preset color settings that are best suited for color management in varied workflows. When you select a preset color setting, InDesign automatically applies default settings to the **Working Spaces** and **Color Management Policies** sections. You can also customize the preset color settings by selecting the **Custom** option.

In the **Color Settings** dialog box, the **Working Spaces** section provides an intermediate color space that is used to define and edit colors in Adobe applications. You can also set color management policies that specify how the application handles data when an image is opened or imported using this dialog box. The **Description** section in the **Color Settings** dialog box displays information about the color settings.

Mixed RGB and CMYK Workflows

Creative professionals can mix RGB and CMYK content—and their advantages—in a single, safe and accurate workflow using InDesign CS6. Its features let print professionals use their current CMYK workflow and keep CMYK graphics protected, as they add RGB content—increasingly available from digital cameras to high-quality stock image libraries, and more easily repurposed.

A mixed RGB-CMYK color workflow requires a safe approach, to avoid unexpected color conversions and preserve blacks without introducing other colors. Both Illustrator CS6 and InDesign CS6 employ a safe CMYK mode to preserve CMYK color numbers all the way to the final output. In particular, the safe CMYK mode preserves blacks and ensures that they are not accidentally re-separated.

 Access the Checklist tile on your LogicalCHOICE course screen for reference information and job aids on How to Manage Colors

ACTIVITY 9-1
Managing Colors

Data Files

Playbill.indd

Scenario

In order to get the best color output from your printer, you decide to assign the most appropriate color profile considering the paper stock it will be printed on.

1. Navigate to the file **C:\092022Data\Customizing Print Settings\Playbill.indd** and go to page **1**.

2. Select **Edit→Assign Profiles**.

3. In the **Assign Profiles** dialog box, in the **CMYK Profile** section, select **Assign Profile** and in the drop-down menu, select **U.S. Sheetfed Coated v2**.

4. Check the **Preview** check box. Verify that the colors darkened.

5. Select **OK**.

6. Save the file as *My Playbill.indd*

TOPIC B

Preview the Print Output

It is always considered a best practice to review a test print before you hand off to a commercial printer. InDesign features a number of settings so you can get the best idea of how your document will look after being printed. In this topic, you will preview the print output.

Overprint

Overprint is a print technique that makes the topmost color of overlapping shapes transparent. This technique is used to avoid gaps between colors and is supported only by separation devices. While printing, the colors in the overlapping area are blended to form a new color. The **Attributes** panel is used to set up overprinting, and the *Overprint preview* command on the **View** menu is used to preview the overprints. Created overprints can be simulated or discarded using the **Print** dialog box.

Separations

When artwork is given for printing, the printer separates the artwork into four plates—Cyan, Magenta, Yellow, and Black. These four colors combine to print the actual image. The four plates are created using films which are called separations. The process of separating artwork into different colors is called *color separation.*

The Separations Preview Panel

The **Separations Preview** panel enables you to preview the color separation of a file before printing it. This would help you to troubleshoot common printing issues that may occur in commercial printing. You can use the **Ink Limit** option to identify whether the ink limit has exceeded the specified limit and then control the density of the ink, using the options provided in the **Ink Manager**. You can also use the **Ink Manager** to convert spot colors to process inks, so that the image is reproduced accurately. In addition, the **Ink Manager** allows you to specify the desired color and use standard lab values for reproducing spot colors.

Flattening

Flattening is the process that isolates areas where transparent objects overlap other objects. It divides the artwork into components and determines if it can be represented using vector data or if it needs to be rasterized.

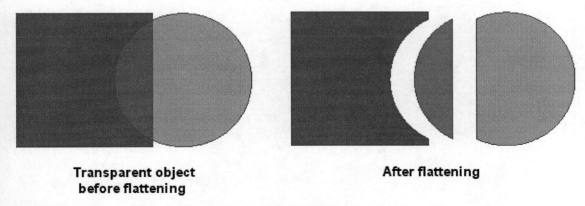

Transparent object before flattening

After flattening

Figure 9-1: An example of a transparency after flattening.

The Flattener Preview Panel

The **Flattener Preview** panel enables you to preview the areas that will be affected by flattening. The options in the **Highlight** drop-down menu enable you to specify the areas to be highlighted. This panel also contains options for refreshing the highlights and selecting a flattener preset for the document. The **Flattener Preview** panel options menu enables you to create, edit, and load flattener presets.

Print Booklet

The **Print Booklet** feature (**File→Print Booklet**) lets you create printer spreads for professional printing. For example, if you're editing an 8-page booklet, the pages appear in sequential order in the layout window. However, in printer spreads, page 2 is positioned next to page 7, so that when the two pages are printed on the same sheet, folded, and collated, the pages end up in the appropriate order. The process of creating printer spreads from layout spreads is called imposition. While imposing pages, you can change settings to adjust spacing between pages, margins, bleed, and creep. The layout of your InDesign document is not affected, because the imposition is all handled in the print stream. No pages are shuffled or rotated in the document.

 Access the Checklist tile on your LogicalCHOICE course screen for reference information and job aids on **How to Preview the Print Output**

ACTIVITY 9-2
Previewing the Print Output

Before You Begin

My Playbill.indd is open.

Scenario

In order to avoid any unpleasant, costly surprises, you decide to preview the print output such as overprint, separations, and flattener within InDesign before you send it out to the printer.

---

1. Preview the document to check the colors and overprint.
   a) Select **View→Overprint Preview**. Overprint Preview should now have a check mark to show it's enabled.
   b) Select **View→Proof Colors** to enable it.
   c) Scroll through the document to verify the quality of the colors.

2. Preview separations.
   a) Select **Window→Output→Separations Preview**.
   b) In the **Separations Preview** panel, in the **View** drop-down list, verify that **Separations** is selected.
   c) Select the toggle visibility eye icon 👁 of **Cyan, Magenta,** and **Black** to view the amount of **Yellow** that will print on each page.
   d) Restore the visibility of **Cyan, Magenta,** and **Black** and close the **Separations Preview** panel.

3. View the transparency of the objects in the document.
   a) Select **Window→Output→Flattener Preview**.
   b) In the **Flattener Preview** panel, in the **Highlight** drop-down list, select **Transparent Objects.**
   c) Verify that the **Scrimdown logo** is highlighted and appears correctly. If necessary, select **Refresh**.
   d) Close the **Flattener Preview** panel group.

4. Save the document.

TOPIC C

Create Print Presets

A time-saving feature you should consider is creating print presets. All your print settings can be saved as a custom preset for future use on similar projects. In this topic, you will create print presets.

Print Presets

Print presets are settings that determine the print output of a file. You can customize the print settings and the type of the printer used to suit your requirements. The saved presets will be available for any document within the application. Print presets can be created either by defining them or by saving the current print settings.

Trapping

When a document page contains multiple colors, more than one ink color has to be used for printing. The inks used must align properly. When inks do not align, gaps may occur between two different colors. This process of filling the gaps between different colors of overlapping objects is called *trapping*.

Ink Manager

The **Ink Manager** dialog box provides control over inks at print output. The output is affected when you make changes to it using the **Ink Manager** and not when colors are defined in the document. For example, when a document includes a spot color, the options of the **Ink Manager** dialog box are used to change the spot color to its equivalent CMYK process color.

 Access the Checklist tile on your LogicalCHOICE course screen for reference information and job aids on How to Create Print Presets

ACTIVITY 9–3
Creating Print Presets

Before You Begin
My Playbill.indd is open.

Scenario
The Romeo & Juliet playbill is ready for the printer. Since this will be the first of many productions at Scrimdown Playhouse requiring a playbill, it seems smart to create a print preset that will keep the look of the playbills consistent.

---

1. Select the printer.
   a) Select **File→Print Presets→Define**.
   b) In the **Print Presets** dialog box, select **New**.
   c) In the **New Print Preset** dialog box, in the **Name** field, type *Scrimdown Playbill* and from the **Printer** drop-down menu, select PostScript ® File.
   d) In the **PPD** drop-down menu, verify that **Adobe PDF 9.0** is selected.

2. Specify the print settings.
   a) In the **General** category, in the **Pages** section, select **Spreads**.
   b) In the **Setup** category, in the **Paper Size** drop-down menu, verify that **Letter** is selected and from the **Page Position** drop-down list, select **Centered**.
   c) In the **Marks and Bleed** category, check the **All Printer's Marks** check box. In the **Bleed and Slug** section, verify that **Use Document Bleed Settings** is unchecked.
   d) If necessary, verify that the **Make all settings the same** button 🔗 is enabled. Change the setting for **Top** to **0.25**.
   e) Select **OK** to save the print settings.
   f) In the **Print Presets** dialog box, select **Save**.
   g) In the **Save Print Presets** dialog box, in the **File name** text box, type *Scrimdown Playbill* and select **Save**.
   h) In the **Print Presets** dialog box, select **OK**.
   i) **Close** the file.

Summary

In this lesson, you previewed the output and created a print preset for your document for use in future similar projects.

Why do you think it's important to take advantage of InDesign's output preview options?

How can creating print presets aid your workflow?

 Note: Check your LogicalCHOICE Course screen for opportunities to interact with your classmates, peers, and the larger LogicalCHOICE online community about the topics covered in this course or other topics you are interested in. From the Course screen you can also access available resources for a more continuous learning experience.

Course Follow-Up

In this course, you learned how to develop layouts for multiple formats and to take advantage of advanced page elements in InDesign CS6. You learned to apply and manage styles and create complex paths. You also learned of all the options you have to make your document interactive and how to work with external files. You learned to manage long documents, publish to other formats and to customize print settings.

What's Next?

Now that you've completed the Adobe® InDesign® CS6 course, you may want to add to your design and media knowledge by taking the following Logical Operations courses:

- *Adobe® Photoshop® CS6: Part 1*
- *Adobe® Photoshop® CS6: Part 2*

You are encouraged to explore InDesign further by actively participating in any of the social media forums set up by your instructor or training administrator through the **Social Media** tile on the LogicalCHOICE Course screen.

A | Productivity Enhancements

Appendix Introduction

The following are enhancements that were introduced in Adobe® InDesign® CS6.

TOPIC A

InDesign Productivity Enhancements

Various enhancements in InDesign are offered to increase productivity.

Split Window

To compare two different layouts in the same document, you can split the active window. Use the two panes to view alternative layouts side by side.

Split Layout View

Use one of these options to view a split layout.

- Select the button in the lower-right corner of the document window.
- Select **Window→Arrange→Split Window**.
- From the **Layout** menu in the **Pages** panel, select **Split Window to Compare Layouts**.

Recently Used Fonts

To find fonts easily and reduce scrolling, view the recently used fonts at the top of the **Font** pop-up and **Type→Fonts** menu.

Specify the number of recent fonts to display under **Edit→Preferences→Type→Number of recent fonts to display**.

By default, the recently used fonts are displayed in chronological order. To display them in alphabetical order, select **Edit→Preferences→Type→Sort Recent Fonts List Alphabetically**.

Align to Key Object

An additional option is available for distributing objects in the **Align** panel.

1. Select the objects to distribute, and in the **Align** panel (**Window→Objects & Layout→Align**) select **Align To Key Object** from the **Align To** list.
2. The key object appears with a thick border. Click another object to select it as the key object.

Save Backward to Earlier Versions

To open an InDesign document in a previous version, or to send it to someone who has not upgraded yet, save the document in the **InDesign Markup Language (IDML)** format. IDML files are supported by InDesign CS4 or later. Features not supported by the earlier version will not work.

The option to save documents to earlier versions is now available from the **Save** and **Save As** dialog boxes.

1. Select **File→Save As**.
2. From the **Save As Type** list, select **InDesign CS4 or later (IDML)**.

Export and Proof Grayscale PDFs

You can now proof and export designs as grayscale PDFs. For example, use this feature to quickly export your layout for grayscale printing. The digital publication remains full color, and you can avoid maintaining separate layouts for grayscale and color outputs.

Use **Proof Setup (View→Proof Setup→Custom)** to specify grayscale proof options, and select a **Dot Gain** or **Gamma** destination. After you've setup the proof, select **View→Proof Colors** to toggle between grayscale and color output.

You can also export a grayscale PDF from within InDesign. All page items, regardless of their original color space, are converted to grayscale while exporting to PDF.

1. Select **File→Export** and select **Adobe PDF (Print)** and select **Save**.
2. In the **Export Adobe PDF** dialog box, select the **Output** tab.
3. Under **Color Conversion,** select **Convert To Destination**.
4. Under **Destination,** select a **Dot Gain** or **Gray Gamma destination**.

 Note: Grayscale destinations are not available under the PDF/X-1a standard. The standard supports only CMYK intents. Similarly, PDF/X-2 or PDF/X-3 standards do not support Gamma Gray destinations.

Complex Calculations in Panels and Dialog Boxes

You can now perform complex calculations within the text fields in panels and dialog boxes. Enter a mathematical expression by using mathematical operators, for example, 120p0/2 + 10.

Export to PNG

To export a selection or a range of pages as an image, select **File→Export** and then select **PNG** from the **Save As Type** list. Use the **Export PNG** dialog box to specify what to export and the export settings.

Export Enhancements

The following are enhancements to the Export feature.

- SWF Export: The **Export SWF** dialog box displays font license information.
- Export For: The **File→Export For** menu has been removed. All supported options are consolidated in the **Save As Type** list in the **Export** dialog box.
- Options for exporting to Buzzword, SVG, and SVG compressed are no longer available.

B | InDesign Language Support

Adobe World-Ready composers and support for open-source HunSpell dictionaries enable you to use several additional languages using InDesign.

Placeholder Text with Specified Alphabet

You can enter placeholder text Roman, Arabic, Hebrew, Chinese among others.

To specify the language of placeholder text, press **Ctrl** when you choose **Type→Fill With Placeholder Text**. In the **Fill Options** dialog box, choose an alphabet and select **OK**.

HunSpell Enhancements

For most languages, InDesign ships with open-source HunSpell dictionaries and HunSpell is the default dictionary provider. You can download and install additional spelling and hyphenation dictionaries for other languages from the OpenOffice website.

To use InDesign with additional languages, select **Edit→Preferences→Dictionary** and then select **HunSpell Info**.

Indic Support

Adobe® World-Ready Composer® (WRC) provides correct word shaping for many of the non-Western scripts, such as Devanagari. Adobe World-Ready composers in the International English version of InDesign, support several Indian languages including Hindi, Marathi, Gujarati, Tamil, Punjabi, Bengali, Telugu, Oriya, Malayalam, and Kannada.

Hunspell spelling and hyphenation dictionaries are included, and so is the Adobe Devanagari font family.

Enable the Adobe World-Ready Composer through a paragraph style (**Paragraph Style→Justification→Composer**) or using the **Paragraph** panel menu.

Set Indic preferences to work on indic scripts, and correctly import content into InDesign.

1. Select **Window→Utilities→Scripts**.
2. Double-click **Indic Preferences.js**.
3. Open a new document or restart InDesign.

Middle Eastern Support

InDesign CS6 is also available in Middle Eastern and North African editions. It adds support for Arabic and Hebrew, and provides several features for working with right-to-left, bi-directional scripts, and other language-specific features. Enhanced functionality includes support for tables in the **Story Editor**, improved Kashida justification, enhanced diacritic positioning, and other text-handling improvements.

See Working with Arabic and Hebrew for more details.

C | Extension Manager CS6

With Extension Manager CS6, you can create, edit, activate, import, and export extension sets. Extension Manager CS6 supports the following:

- User-level extension installation.
- Search and filter extensions.
- MXP to ZXP conversion.
- Extension dependency support.
- Installing extensions when multiple languages of a product are installed.
- Display additional extension information.

D | Adobe InDesign CS6 ACE Certification Exam Objectives

Selected Logical Operations courseware addresses Adobe Certified Expert (ACE) certification skills for Adobe InDesign CS6. The following table indicates where Adobe InDesign CS6 skills that map to Adobe Certified Expert (ACE) certification objectives are covered in the Logical Operations Adobe CS6 series of courses.

Objective Domain	Covered In
1. Layout a Document	
1.1 Creating a new document	Part 1
1.2 Navigating and viewing documents	Part 1
1.3 Constructing a flexible foundation for multi-page document	Part 2, Topic 2-A
1.4 Precisely position objects on a page	Part 1
1.5 Modify and transform objects	Part 1
1.6 Ensure the consistency of objects' formatting throughout a document or publication	Part 2, Lesson 3; Part 1
1.7 Building documents for alternate layouts and print sizes	Part 2, Topic 1-A
1.8 Creating data-driven documents	Part 2, Topic 5-B
2. Working with Text	
2.1 Create and position text in a frame and on a path	Part 2, Topic 4-A; Part 1
2.2 Managing text flow	Part 1
2.3 Importing and editing text	Part 1
2.4 Applying formatting manually and automatically	Part 1
2.5 Inserting special characters	Part 2, Topic 6-B
2.6 Creating tables	Part 1
2.7 Adding long document features	Part 2, Lesson 7
3. Managing Graphics	
3.1 Placing and altering graphics	Part 1

Objective Domain	Covered In
3.2 Working with linked files	Part 2, Topic 1-B
3.3 Adjusting graphic formatting and display	Part 1
4. Understanding Color and Transparency	
4.1 Creating and applying colors	Part 1
4.2 Working with gradients	Part 1
4.3 Applying transparency	Part 2, Topic 2-C
4.4 Color and ink management	Part 2, Topic 9-A
5. Building Interactive Documents	
5.1 Adding interactive objects and behaviors	Part 2, Topic 6-C
5.2 Adjusting interactive behaviors	Part 2, Topic 6-C
5.3 Previewing and exporting interactive documents	Part 2, Topic 6-C
6. Preparing Documents for Final Output	
6.1 Preflighting documents	Part 1
6.2 Exporting PDF for print output	Part 2, Topic 8-A; Part1
6.3 Printing documents	Part 2, Lesson 9; Part 1

E New Features in Adobe InDesign CS6

The following table describes the new features available in Adobe InDesign CS6 and where those features are covered in the InDesign CS6 courses.

Feature	Adobe InDesign CS6: Part 1	Adobe InDesign CS6: Part 2
Alternate Layouts		Lesson 1, Topic A
Liquid Layouts		Lesson 1, Topic A
Linked Content		Lesson 1, Topic B
Digital Publishing		Lesson 1, Topic A
		Lesson 9, Topics B, C, D
EPUB and HTML5		Lesson 9, Topic D
Interactivity		Lesson 7, Topics A, C
Productivity Enhancements	Appendix B	Appendix B
Language Support		Appendix C
Extension Manager CS6		Appendix D

Lesson Labs

Lesson labs are provided for certain lessons as additional learning resources for this course. Lesson labs are developed for selected lessons within a course in cases when they seem most instructionally useful as well as technically feasible. In general, labs are supplemental, optional unguided practice and may or may not be performed as part of the classroom activities. Your instructor will consider setup requirements, classroom timing, and instructional needs to determine which labs are appropriate for you to perform, and at what point during the class. If you do not perform the labs in class, your instructor can tell you if you can perform them independently as self-study, and if there are any special setup requirements.

Lesson Lab 1–1
Creating Documents for Multiple Formats

Activity Time: 10 minutes

Data Files
Playbill Cover Lab.indd

Scenario
The Scrimdown Playhouse marketing department is developing an iPad application and would like to feature the covers of some of the playbills from the Shakespeare festival.

1. Navigate to the folder **C:\092022Data\Creating Documents for Multiple Formats** and open the file **Playbill Cover Lab.indd**.

2. Define **Liquid Layout Rules**.
   a) Shakespeare image can resize and remain bleeding off the left and bottom edges.
   b) Scrimdown Playhouse logo should not resize and should remain the same distance from the right edge.
   c) Green rectangle should resize and keep the same distance from both the right and left edges as well as the top edge.

3. In **Document Setup,** change the **Intent** to **Digital Publishing** and verify that the **Page Size** is set to **iPad.** Verify that **Orientation** is set to **Portrait.**

4. Make manual layout adjustments to the objects. Resize text as necessary.

5. Create an alternate layout for a horizontal orientation.

6. Make manual layout adjustments to the objects. Resize text as necessary.

7. Save the file as *My Playbill Cover Lab.indd* and close the file.

Lesson Lab 2–1
Managing Advanced Page Elements

Activity Time: 10 minutes

Data Files

Sports Brochure Lesson 2 Lab.indd, footprints.tif

Scenario

In an effort to make the brochure for My Footprint Sports more fun and whimsical, you decide to add a footprint icon to the bottom of each page near the page number.

---

1. Navigate to the folder **C:\092022Data\Managing Advanced Page Elements** and open the file **Sports Brochure Lesson 2 Lab.indd**.

2. Open the **A-Master** spread.

3. Place the graphic **C:\092022Data\Managing Advanced Page Elements\footprints.tif**.

4. Resize the footprint to a height of *.3 in* and position it to the right of the text "Keep a running list" on the left page and to the left side of the text on the right page.

5. Open the spread **2-3** and review the placement of the footprint graphic. Open page **4** and verify the graphic on that page as well.

6. Save the file as *My Sports Brochure Lesson 2 Lab.indd* and close it.

Lesson Lab 4–1
Building Complex Paths

Activity Time: 10 minutes

Data Files
Nursery Postcard Lesson 4.indd

Scenario
You need to create an alternate version of the Greene City Nursery School postcard that emphasizes the upcoming 25th anniversary year. In keeping with the child-centric images, you decide to customize the type for this version.

1. Navigate to the folder **C:\092022Data\Building Complex Paths** and open the file **Nursery Postcard Lesson 4 Lab.indd**.

2. Select the text **25** and create outlines. Adjust the anchor points on the resulting path so the text appears more playful in style.

3. Draw a Bézier path in the shape of a curve and place it around the top left corner of the **2** path.

4. On this Bézier path, input the text *Celebrating* in **18 pt Times New Roman**.

5. Save the file as *My Nursery Postcard Lesson 4 Lab.indd* and close the file.

Lesson Lab 5-1
Managing External Files

Activity Time: 10 minutes

Data Files

Application Response Letter Lab.indd, applicants.csv

Scenario

Greene City Nursery School recently posted a job for a new Pre-K teacher. In order to personalize the process, the board decided to send response letters. It is your responsibility to personalize the form letter that will be sent to each of the applicants.

---

1. Navigate to the folder **C:\092022Data\Managing External Files** and open the file **Application Response Letter Lab.indd.**

2. In the **Data Merge** panel options menu, choose **Select Data Source** and browse to the file **C:\092022Data\Managing External Files\applicants.csv.**

3. Just below the text "To:" add placeholders for **Name, Street, City,** and **State,** each on its own line.

4. After the text "**Dear,**" add a placeholder for **Name,** and then type a **,** (comma).

5. Create the merged document.

6. Review the merged document and then save it as *Personalized Application Response Letter.indd* and close the file.

7. Save and close the file **Application Response Letter Lab .indd.**

Glossary

absolute page numbering
A type of page numbering where the pages are numbered sequentially.

anchored object
Any object that has a link to a text frame.

book
A file that is comprised of more than one document.

Bézier path
A path that contains one or more anchor points with direction handles to adjust the size of the path.

clipping path
A path that is used to hide the outside areas of an image and make the inside area visible.

color management
The process of controlling software and hardware to match colors between devices such as a computer monitor and a printer.

color separation
The process of breaking up the different colors in an artwork onto different printing plates.

compound path
A path that contains more than one path and intersects to form a hole.

data merge
An InDesign feature that can be used to create data by merging data from two different files.

document pages
InDesign pages that are created for laying out text and graphical objects.

embedded clipping path
A clipping path that is imported from other applications.

flattening
A process that divides transparent objects into vector-based and raster-based areas in an artwork.

footnote
A note that is associated with text on a page and is placed at the bottom of the page.

hyperlink
A link that enables users to move to another location.

hyphenation
A process of inserting hyphens in between the syllables of a word so that when the text is justified, maximum space is utilized.

index
A list of words in a document and their associated page numbers.

inline graphic
A graphic that appears along with the text, usually with the description.

interactive document
A document that allows you to navigate to linked pages.

justification
A paragraph option to control the spacing between letters of a word.

keep options
A feature that allows you to keep lines of a paragraph together and specify break links in a line.

kern pairs
A pair of letters with spacing already adjusted.

kerning
A character format used to adjust the space between specific letter pairs.

keywords
Text that can be assigned to files for identification.

layer comps
Different forms of an image that are stored in a file.

layered file
A file that has more than one layer.

library
A storage location which is mainly used for reusing components.

master page
A virtual page that appears by default whenever a new document is created and where you can store objects or items which can be applied to all the pages in a document.

metadata
A description based on the properties of data.

metrics kerning
A character format used to adjust the space between kern pairs.

nested style
A style that allows to apply character-level formatting to specific ranges of text within a paragraph.

optical kerning
A character format used to adjust the space between characters of different font or size.

overprint
A technique that displays the topmost color of overlapping shapes as transparent, thereby displaying the corner edges of the areas underneath.

overprint preview
A command that is used to identify problems during printing.

pagination
The consecutive numbering or organization of content in a document according to the specified settings.

PDF
(Portable Document Format) An open file format specification which is accessed by multiple users across different platforms because of its ability to retain the original layout and print qualities in its native file format.

Presentation mode
A view that displays an active document as a presentation.

print preset
Print job settings saved to determine the print output of a file.

process color
A color that is a combination of any or all of the standard colors: cyan, magenta, yellow, and black.

scaling
A character format used to specify the height and width of text.

section
A portion of the document that is meant for holding document items such as an index or a preface.

section page numbering

A type of page numbering where you specify the page number preceded by a section name.

spot color

A color that allows you to print objects with a single ink.

stack

A feature that allows you to group all images in a single thumbnail.

style override

The format applied to text that is already formatted using a style.

style redefining

A feature that allows you to change the attributes of an existing style.

table of contents

An item that helps users find information quickly.

tracking

Adjusting the space between the letters within a selection.

transparency

An effect created by adjusting the opacity of an object.

trapping

The process of expanding objects to fill gaps between different colors of overlapping objects.

type outline

An outline created form an existing path where you can adjust the shape of the type to a wide range of sizes.

widows and orphans

Words or single lines of text that are separated from the rest of the paragraph.

XHTML

(eXtensible Hypertext Markup Language) A HTML markup language that is defined as an XML application.

Index